McGraw-Hill Education's

Medical Spanish Visual Phrasebook

Neil Bobenhouse, MHA, EMT-P

New York Chicago San Francisco Athens London Madrid
Mexico City Milan New Delhi Singapore Sydney Toronto

1 2 3 4 5 6 7 8 9 10 CTP/CTP 1 0 9 8 7 6 5 4 3

ISBN	978-1-260-02672-6
MHID	1-260-02672-8
e-ISBN	978-0-07-180889-7
e-MHID	0-07-180889-2

Library of Congress Control Number 2012948445

NOTICE

This book is not intended to provide medical advice or to substitute for the advice of a licensed medical professional, and readers should consult an appropriate medical practitioner for all matters relating to their health. Medicine is an ever-changing science. As new research and clinical experience broaden our knowledge, changes in treatment and drug therapy are required. The authors and the publisher of this work have checked with sources believed to be reliable in their efforts to provide information that is complete and generally in accord with the standards accepted at the time of publication. However, in view of the possibility of human error or changes in medical sciences, neither the authors nor the publisher nor any other party who has been involved in the preparation or publication of this work warrants that the information contained herein is in every respect accurate or complete, and they disclaim all responsibility for any errors or omissions or for the results obtained from use of the information contained in this work. Readers are encouraged to confirm the information contained herein with other sources. For example and in particular, readers are advised to check the product information sheet included in the package of each drug they plan to administer to be certain that any information contained in this work is accurate and that changes have not been made in the recommended dose or in the contraindications for administration.

Credits appear on page 152

McGraw-Hill Education products are available at special quantity discounts to use as premiums and sales promotions or for use in corporate training programs. To contact a representative, please visit the Contact Us pages at www.mhprofessional.com.

This book is printed on acid-free paper.

About the Phrasebook

McGraw-Hill Education's Medical Spanish Visual Phrasebook is a communication aid specifically designed for EMTs, paramedics, nurses, physicians, and other healthcare providers who need to communicate with non-English-speaking patients. This book is a valuable bridge for healthcare providers to better understand their patients before proper translation services can be accessed. You do not need to know any language other than English to successfully use this book. All foreign language elements are presented with visual images or phrased as yes-no questions. Non-English speaking patients can point to the relevant images or respond to simple questions with a nod of the head or a simple "yes" or "no" in order to communicate essential information. The book is designed to be useful from intake to discharge. Primary assessments ask general questions while the secondary assessments contain in-depth questions for specific specialties. These assessments feature the most basic words and phrases that allow you to get essential information from patients. Secondary assessments are divided into three sections: Acute History, Procedural, and Past History. Procedural sections contain statements that may be useful when examining a patient or communicating what might be happening.

As with any medical assessment, a subjective account must be considered with vital signs and other objective measures. THIS PHRASEBOOK IS NOT A DIAGNOSTIC DEVICE AND CANNOT DIAGNOSE MEDICAL CONDITIONS. THIS PHRASEBOOK IS STRICTLY A TRANSLATION AID. It must be understood that no translation is absolute and perfect. All translations were written with a general audience in mind.

How to use This Phrasebook

The sequence of questions is intended to flow with a normal assessment but written to be stand alone questions as well. Questions were ordered from "head to toe," "onset, provocation, quality, radiation, strength, time," and increasing focus. Secondary Assessment sections were focused on immediate signs/symptoms, procedures that would begin shortly after, and long-term history. This general format is amended in certain areas as needed.

Contents

CONTENTS

SECONDARY ASSESSMENT AND HISTORY

Contents

Contents

Hola, soy un(a) profesional de la salud. No hablo español.
Hello, I am a healthcare professional. I do not speak Spanish.

Respóndame solo sí no o no lo sé .
Respond to me "yes," "no" or "I don't know."

¿Está usted aquí por un problema médico o de enfermedad?

Are you here for a medical problem or sickness?

¿Está usted aquí debido a una lesión física?

Are you here because of a physical injury?

Por favor, anote su nombre claramente.
Please write your name clearly.

_____

Por favor, anote la fecha actual claramente.
Please write the current date clearly.

___ / ___ / ___
DÍA   MES   AÑO

Por favor, anote su dirección de correo claramente.
Please write your mailing address clearly.

_____

Calle (Street)   **Apartamento** (Apt. #)

_____

Ciudad (City)   **Estado** (State)   **Código Postal** (ZIP)

DEMOGRAPHICS

2

Por favor, anote su número de teléfono claramente.
Please write your phone number clearly.

(_____) _____ - _____

Por favor, anote su número de seguro social.
Please write your Social Security number.

_____ - _____ - _____

Por favor, permítame su licencia de conducir o identificación Estatal.
Tengo que sacarle una copia y se la devolveré en breve.
Please give me your driver's license or State ID. I need to make a copy
of it and will return it to you shortly.

¿Tiene seguro médico?
Do you have medical insurance?

Por favor, permítame su tarjeta de seguro. Tengo que sacarle
una copia y se la devolveré en breve.
Please give me your insurance card. I need to make a copy of it and will
return it to you shortly.

¿Se le considera legalmente hombre o mujer?
Are you legally male or female?

 Hombre
Male

 Mujer
Female

¿Tiene empleo?
Are you employed?

Por favor, anote el nombre del lugar donde trabaja.
Please write the name of your place of work.

Por favor, párese en la báscula.
Please step on this scale.

¿Cuál es su estado civil?
What is your marital status?

 Soltero(a)
Single

 Divorciado(a)
Divorced

 Casado(a)
Married

 Viudo(a)
Widowed

¿Necesita ayuda para bañarse, comer, vestirse o cuidar de su hogar?
Do you need help with bathing, eating, dressing, or taking care of your household?

¿Se encuentra usted en una relación donde corre peligro físico o emocional?
Are you in a harmful physical or emotional relationship?

DEMOGRAPHICS

4

¿Tiene redactado un documento de instrucciones anticipadas?

Do you have an advanced directive?

¿Bebe más de cinco bebidas alcohólicas al día?

Do you drink more than five alcoholic drinks a day?

 Sí
Yes

 No
No

 Dejé el trago
I quit

Por favor, indique el tipo de bebida alcohólica que normalmente bebe.

Please indicate type of alcohol you normally drink.

 Cerveza
Beer

 Whiskey
Whiskey

 Vodka
Vodka

 Bourbon
Bourbon

 Vino
Wine

 Otra
Other

 Ginebra
Gin

¿Fuma cigarrillos o utiliza productos de tabaco?

Do you smoke cigarettes or use tobacco products?

 Sí
Yes

 No
No

 Dejé de fumar
I quit

¿Ha tenido un resultado positivo en la prueba de la tuberculosis?

Have you had a positive test for tuberculosis?

¿Utiliza alguna droga ilícita o medicamentos que
no fueron prescritos para usted?

Do you use any illicit drugs/medications that are not prescribed to you?

 Sí
Yes

 No
No

 Dejé las drogas
I quit

Por favor, indique qué tipo de drogas utiliza.
Please indicate what type of drugs you use.

 Cocaína
Cocaine

 Marihuana
Marijuana

 Éxtasis
Ecstasy

 Metanfetaminas
Methamphetamines

 Heroína
Heroin

 Otra
Other

 LSD/ "ácido"
LSD/"acid"

Por favor, indique de qué forma usa estas drogas.
Please indicate in which form you use these drugs.

 **Inyectada por
vía intravenosa**
Inject intravenously

 Aspirada por la nariz
Snort

 Introducida por vía rectal
Insert rectally

 **Por vía oral en forma
de píldora**
Swallow in pill form

 Fumada
Smoke

 Otra
Other

DEMOGRAPHICS

6

¿Usa gafas y/o contactos?
Do you wear glasses and/or contacts?

¿Usa aparatos auditivos?
Do you wear hearing aids?

¿Cómo describiría su apetito?
How would you describe your appetite?

 Normal
Normal

 Más de lo normal
Greater than normal

 Anormal
Abnormal

 Menos de lo normal
Less than normal

 Inconsistente
Inconsistent

¿Cómo describiría su dieta?
How would you describe your diet?

 Saludable
Healthy

 Poco saludable
Somewhat unhealthy

 Más o menos saludable
Somewhat healthy

 No saludable
Unhealthy

 Ni saludable ni no saludable
Neither healthy nor unhealthy

¿La razón por la cual está aquí está relacionada con el trabajo?
Is the reason why you are here work related?

MEDICAL ASSESSMENT

Hola, soy un(a) profesional de la salud. No hablo español.

Hello, I am a healthcare professional. I do not speak Spanish.

Respóndame solo sí o no .

Only respond to me "yes" or "no."

¿Actualmente tiene o ha tenido recientemente los siguientes síntomas?

Do you currently have/recently had the following symptoms?

Spanish			English
Dolor abdominal			Abdominal pain
Dolores musculares			Aches
Dolor de espalda			Back pain
Nacidos o abscesos			Boil or abscess
Dolor en los huesos o en las articulaciones			Bone or joint pain
Dolor en el pecho			Chest pain
Escalofríos			Chills
Diarrea			Diarrhea
Dificultad para tragar			Difficulty swallowing
Dificultad para hablar			Difficulty talking
Dificultad para caminar y/o moverse			Difficulty walking/moving
Mareos			Dizziness
Dolor en los oídos			Earache

MEDICAL ASSESSMENT

8

Spanish			English
Dolor en los ojos	✓	✗	Eye pain
Fiebre	✓	✗	A fever
Dolor en los genitales	✓	✗	Genital pain
Dolor de cabeza	✓	✗	A headache
Problemas de la audición	✓	✗	Hearing problems
Dolor en la pierna	✓	✗	Leg pain
Náuseas	✓	✗	Nausea
Secreción del pezón	✓	✗	Nipple discharge
Entumecimiento u hormigueo	✓	✗	Numbness or tingling
Sangrado nasal	✓	✗	A nose bleed
Erupción	✓	✗	Rash
Sangrado rectal	✓	✗	Rectal bleeding
Falta de aire / dificultad para respirar	✓	✗	Shortness of breath
Dolor en el hombro	✓	✗	Shoulder pain
Cambio de color en la piel	✓	✗	Skin color change
Dolor de garganta	✓	✗	A sore throat
Dolor de estómago	✓	✗	Stomach pain

MEDICAL ASSESSMENT

¿Actualmente tiene o ha tenido recientemente los siguientes síntomas?

Do you currently have/recently had the following symptoms?

Hinchazón	✓	✗	Swelling
Dificultad para orinar	✓	✗	Urination difficulty
Problemas de visión	✓	✗	Vision problems
Vómito	✓	✗	Vomiting
Debilidad	✓	✗	Weakness

¿Los síntomas comenzaron hoy?

Did your symptoms begin today?   ✓   ✗

Sírvase indicar a qué hora comenzaron los síntomas hoy.

Please indicate what time your symptoms began today.

AM	1	2	3	4	5	6	7	8	9	10	11	12
PM	1	2	3	4	5	6	7	8	9	10	11	12

¿Los síntomas comenzaron esta semana?

Did your symptoms begin this week?   ✓   ✗

Sírvase indicar cuantos días han pasado desde el inicio de los síntomas.

Please indicate how many days have passed since your symptoms began.

1   2   3   4   5   6   7

MEDICAL ASSESSMENT

10

¿Los síntomas comenzaron hace más de una semana?
Did your symptoms begin longer than a week ago?

Sírvase indicar cuantas semanas han pasado desde el inicio de los síntomas.
Please indicate how many weeks have passed since your symptoms began.

| **SEMANAS** | 1 | 2 | 3 | 4 | 5 | 6 | 7 | 8 | 9 | 10 | > |
| WEEKS | | | | | | | | | | | |

| **MESES** | 1 | 2 | 3 | 4 | 5 | 6 | 7 | 8 | 9 | 10 | > |
| MONTHS | | | | | | | | | | | |

¿Ha experimentado estos síntomas previamente?
Have you experienced these symptoms previously?

¿Tiene estos síntomas varias veces?
Do you have these symptoms repeatedly?

¿Cuándo fue la última vez que tomó sus medicamentos?
When did you last take your prescribed medications?

| **DÍAS** | 1 | 2 | 3 | 4 | 5 | 6 | 7 | > |
| DAYS | | | | | | | | |

¿Cuándo fue la última vez que comió?
When is the last time you had food?

| **DÍAS** | 1 | 2 | 3 | 4 | 5 | 6 | 7 | > |
| DAYS | | | | | | | | |

¿Puede comer alimentos sólidos sin dificultad?
Can you eat solid foods without difficulty?

¿Puede beber líquidos sin dificultad?
Can you drink liquids without difficulty?

PHYSICAL ASSESSMENT

Hola, soy un(a) profesional de la salud. No hablo español.

Hello, I am a healthcare professional. I do not speak Spanish.

Por favor, señale (en este dibujo de una persona) donde tiene dolor.

Please point (on this picture of a person) to where you have pain.

Por favor, indique (en la siguiente escala) la intensidad de su dolor.

Please point (on this scale) to rate your pain.

No hay dolor   Dolor moderado   Dolor intenso

¿Cuándo ocurrió la lesión?
When did your injury occur?

MINUTOS Minutes	10	20	30	40	50	60					
HORAS Hours	2	4	6	8	10	12	14	16	18	20	22
DÍAS Days	1	2	3	4	5	6	7	8	9	10	>
MESES Months	1	2	3	4	5	6	7	8	9	10	>
AÑOS Years	1	2	3	4	5	6	7	8	9	10	>

¿Qué causó esta lesión?
What caused this injury?

- **Fui agredido**
  Assault
- **Un accidente de vehículo todo terreno o de moto**
  ATV/Motorcycle accident
- **Un accidente de carro**
  Car accident
- **Estrujado o apretado**
  Crush
- **Una caída**
  Fall
- **Lesiones deportivas**
  Sports injury
- **Otro**
  Other
- **No lo sé**
  I don't know

¿Perdió el conocimiento?
Did you lose consciousness?

¿Cómo describiría el dolor?
How would you describe your pain?

✓ **Persistente**
Aching

✓ **Abrazador**
Burning

✓ **Devastador**
Crushing

✓ **Sordo**
Dull

✓ **Insistente**
Nagging

✓ **Agudo**
Sharp

✓ **Fulgurante**
Shooting

✓ **Lacerante**
Stabbing

¿Vacunado contra el tétano en los últimos 5 años?
Have you had a tetanus shot within the past 5 years?   ? ✓ ✕

¿Cuándo fue la última vez que tomó sus medicamentos?
When did you last take your prescribed medications?

DÍAS   1   2   3   4   5   6   7   >

¿Cuándo fue la última vez que comió?
When is the last time you had food?

DÍAS   1   2   3   4   5   6   7   >

¿Puede comer alimentos sólidos sin dificultad?
Can you eat solid foods without difficulty?

¿Puede beber líquidos sin dificultad?
Can you drink liquids without difficulty?

EXPANDED QUESTIONS

14

ASSAULT

....

¿Con qué lo atacaron?
What were you attacked with?

 Con un objeto contundente
Blunt object

Otro
Other

A puños
Fist

No lo sé.
I don't know.

Con puñal
Knife

¿Cuántas veces?
How many times?

1   2   3   4   5   >   ?

ATV/MOTORCYCLE ACCIDENT

....

¿Usted estaba usando casco?
Were you wearing a helmet?

¿Usted fue expulsado de su vehículo?
Were you ejected off your vehicle?

¿Ha tomado bebidas alcohólicas el día de hoy?
Have you been drinking alcohol today?

¿Ha usado drogas recreativas el día de hoy?
Have you been using recreational drugs today?

....

MOTOR VEHICLE CRASH

¿Usted recuerda lo que sucedió?
Do you remember what happened?

¿Usted tenía el cinturón de seguridad abrochado?
Were you wearing a seatbelt?

¿Dónde estaba usted sentado?
Where were you sitting?

¿Se inflaron las bolsas de aire?
Did your airbags deploy?

¿Tiene entumecimiento u hormigueo en los brazos?
Do you have numbness or tingling in your arms?

¿Tiene debilidad en los brazos?
Do you have weakness in your arms?

EXPANDED QUESTIONS

16

¿Tiene entumecimiento u hormigueo en las piernas?
Do you have numbness or tingling in your legs?

¿Tiene debilidad en las piernas?
Do you have weakness in your legs?

¿Perdió el conocimiento?
Did you lose consciousness?

¿Salió del carro por sus propios medios?
Did you get out of the car on your own?

¿Le duele el cuello o espalda?
Does your neck or back hurt?

¿Ha estado tomando alcohol?
Have you been drinking alcohol?

¿Ha estado utilizando drogas ilícitas?
Have you been using illicit drugs?

¿Recuerda lo que pasó antes del accidente?
Do you remember what happened before the crash?

¿Recuerda lo que pasó después del accidente?
Do you remember what happened after the crash?

FALL

¿De qué altura se cayó?
From what height did you fall?

Sentado
Sitting

De pie
Standing

Edificio de 1 piso
One story

Edificio de 2 pisos o más
Two stories or more

¿Se golpeó la cabeza?
Did you hit your head?

¿Perdió el conocimiento?
Did you lose consciousness?

¿Tiene entumecimiento u hormigueo en los brazos?
Do you have numbness or tingling in your arms?

¿Tiene debilidad en los brazos?
Do you have weakness in your arms?

¿Tiene entumecimiento u hormigueo en las piernas?
Do you have numbness or tingling in your legs?

¿Tiene debilidad en las piernas?
Do you have weakness in your legs?

EXPANDED QUESTIONS

18
SPORTS INJURY

¿Qué deporte estaba practicando cuando se lesionó?
What sport were you injured playing?

- **Fútbol Americano**
  American Football
- **Baloncesto**
  Basketball
- **Béisbol**
  Baseball
- **Fútbol**
  Soccer
- **Hockey**
  Hockey
- **Tenis**
  Tennis

- **Patinaje Sobre Ruedas**
  Rollerskating
- **Skateboarding**
  Skateboarding
- **Esquí**
  Skiing
- **Snowboard**
  Snowboarding
- **Levantamiento de Pesas**
  Weightlifting
- **Otro**
  Other

¿Usted estaba usando casco?
Were you wearing a helmet?

¿Estaba usando un suspensorio atlético para los genitales?
Were you wearing an athletic supporter for your genitalia?

¿Perdió el conocimiento?
Did you lose consciousness?

ALLERGIES

Hola, soy un(a) profesional de la salud. No hablo español.

Hello, I am a healthcare professional. I do not speak Spanish.

Respóndame solo sí no o no lo sé ?.

Respond to me "yes," "no" or "I don't know."

ALLERGIES

¿Tiene alergia a algún medicamento?
Do you have allergies to any medications?

¿Tiene alergia a alguna comida?
Do you have allergies to any foods?

¿Sufre de alergia estacional?
Do you have seasonal allergies?

¿Es usted alérgico al látex?
Are you allergic to latex?

MEDICATIONS

¿Usted toma medicamentos prescritos en casa?
Do you take prescribed medications at home?

¿Tiene sus medicamentos aquí?
Do you have your medications with you?

Por favor, muéstreme sus medicamentos.
Please show me your medications.

PAST MEDICAL HISTORY

20

Hola, soy un(a) profesional de la salud. No hablo español.

Hello, I am a healthcare professional. I do not speak Spanish.

Respóndame solo sí o no .

Only respond to me "yes" or "no."

PAST MEDICAL HISTORY

¿Usted toma medicamentos prescritos en casa?

Do you take prescribed medications at home?

¿Tiene historial de?:

Do you have a history of:

Ingestión accidental			*Accidental ingestions*
Artritis			*Arthritis*
Asma			*Asthma*
Fibrilación auricular			*Atrial fibrillation*
Trastorno de coagulación de la sangre			*Blood clotting disorder*
Bronquitis			*Bronchitis*
Cáncer			*Cancer*
Parálisis cerebral			*Cerebral palsy*
Varicela			*Chicken pox*
Insuficiencia renal crónica			*Chronic renal failure*

PAST MEDICAL HISTORY

Complicaciones de la circuncisión	✓	✗	Circumcision complications
Labio y paladar leporino	✓	✗	Cleft lip/palate
Insuficiencia cardíaca congestiva (ICC)	✓	✗	Congestive heart failure (CHF)
Cortes, heridas, contusiones o heridas que no se han curado	✓	✗	Cuts, wounds, abrasions, or sores that have not healed
Problemas dentales	✓	✗	Dental problems
Condiciones dermatológicas	✓	✗	Dermatological conditions
Diabetes Mellitus Tipo 1 (insulinodependiente)	✓	✗	Diabetes mellitus Type 1 (IDDM)
Diabetes Mellitus Tipo 2	✓	✗	Diabetes mellitus Type 2
Enfisema	✓	✗	Emphysema
Disfunción del sistema endocrino	✓	✗	Endocrine system dysfunction
Epiglotitis	✓	✗	Epiglottitis
Reflujo gastroesofágico	✓	✗	Gastric esophageal reflux disease (GERD)
Problemas genitales (hombres)	✓	✗	Genital problems (Male)
Problemas ginecológicos	✓	✗	Gynecological problems
VIH/SIDA	✓	✗	HIV/AIDs
Problemas de la audición	✓	✗	Hearing problems

PAST MEDICAL HISTORY

22

Spanish			English
Infarto	✓	✗	*Heart attack*
Hemofilia	✓	✗	*Hemophilia*
Hepatitis A	✓	✗	*Hepatitis A*
Hepatitis B	✓	✗	*Hepatitis B*
Hepatitis C	✓	✗	*Hepatitis C*
Alta presión	✓	✗	*High blood pressure*
Problemas del sistema inmunológico	✓	✗	*Immune system conditions*
Problemas intestinales	✓	✗	*Intestinal conditions*
Meningitis	✓	✗	*Meningitis*
Mononucleosis	✓	✗	*Mononucleosis*
Enterocolitis necrotizante	✓	✗	*Necrotizing enterocolitis*
Trasplante de órganos	✓	✗	*Organ transplant*
Agresión física o sexual	✓	✗	*Physical/ sexual assault*
Neumonía	✓	✗	*Pneumonia*
Problemas psiquiátricos	✓	✗	*Psychiatric conditions*
Fisioterapia para una lesión	✓	✗	*Physical therapy for an injury*

PAST MEDICAL HISTORY

Español	✓	✗	English
Embolia pulmonar	✓	✗	Pulmonary embolism
Cirugía reciente	✓	✗	Recent surgery
Dermatofitosis / pie de atleta	✓	✗	Ringworm/ athlete's foot
El VSR/Bronquiolitis	✓	✗	RSV/Bronchiolitis
Escabiosis	✓	✗	Scabies
Escoliosis	✓	✗	Scoliosis
Convulsiones o problemas neurológicos	✓	✗	Seizures or neurological conditions
Convulsiones febriles	✓	✗	Febrile seizures
Crisis drepanocítica	✓	✗	Sickle cell crises
Espina bífida	✓	✗	Spina bifida
Taquicardia supraventricular (SVT)	✓	✗	Supra ventricular tachycardia (SVT)
Candidiasis bucal / infecciones causadas por levaduras candidas	✓	✗	Thrush/ yeast infections
Fístulas transesofágicas	✓	✗	Transesophageal fistulas
Úlceras o problemas estomacales	✓	✗	Ulcers or stomach conditions
Problemas de la vista	✓	✗	Vision problems

24

Blood pressure

. . . .

Le voy a tomar la presión arterial. Tal vez sienta incomodidad en el brazo pero solo por un momento.

I am going to take your blood pressure. Your arm may be briefly uncomfortable but only for a moment.

Blood Sample

. . . .

Tengo que utilizar una jeringa para obtener una muestra de sangre. Tal vez le arda brevemente pero esto es importante hacerlo para nosotros entender mejor cómo ayudarlo.

I need to use a needle to get a blood sample. This may sting briefly, but is important so we can better understand how to help you.

Catheter

. . . .

Tengo que colocarle un tubo en la vejiga. Esto va a ser incómodo momentáneamente.

I need to put a tube in your bladder. This will be uncomfortable for a moment.

EKG

. . . .

Voy a colocarle unos adhesivos en los brazos y/o el tórax para medir la actividad eléctrica del corazón. Por favor no se mueva. Esto no le va a doler.

I am going to put some stickers on your arms and/or chest to measure the electrical activity of your heart. Please stay very still. This will not hurt.

. . . .

IV

Voy a colocarle suero. Va a sentir una punzada brevemente pero esto es importante hacerlo para poder administrarle medicamentos.

I am going to start an IV. This may sting briefly, but is important so we can give you medication.

RESPIRATORY

Tengo que escuchar los pulmones. Por favor, respire normalmente.

I need to listen to your lungs. Please breathe normally.

TEMPERATURE

Le voy a tomar la temperatura con un termómetro. Por favor, abra la boca.

I am going to take your temperature with a thermometer.
Please open your mouth.

URINE SAMPLE

Por favor, orine en este vaso. Cuando haya terminado, por favor tápelo y entrégueme la muestra.

Please urinate in this cup. When you are finished please secure the lid on top and give the sample to me.

CARDIOLOGY

26

Hola, soy un(a) profesional de la salud. No hablo español.

Hello, I am a healthcare professional. I do not speak Spanish.

Respóndame solo sí o no .

Only respond to me "yes" or "no."

ACUTE CARDIAC HISTORY

¿Siente dolor en el pecho?

Do you have chest pain?

Por favor, señale (en este dibujo de una persona) donde tiene dolor.

Please point (on this picture of a person) to where you have pain.

¿Cuándo comenzó el dolor?
When did your pain begin?

MINUTOS	10	20	30	40	50	60				
MINUTES										

HORAS	2	4	6	8	10	12	14	16	18	20	22
HOURS											

DÍAS	1	2	3	4	5	6	7	8	9	10	>
DAYS											

¿Qué estaba haciendo cuando empezó el dolor?
What were you doing when the pain began?

- ✓ **Estaba parado**
  Standing
- ✓ **Sentado**
  Sitting
- ✓ **Corriendo**
  Running
- ✓ **Caminando**
  Walking
- ✓ **Montando bicicleta**
  Riding bicycle
- ✓ **Levantando objetos pesados**
  Lifting heavy objects

- ✓ **Durmiendo**
  Sleeping
- ✓ **Comiendo**
  Eating
- ✓ **Fumando**
  Smoking
- ✓ **Actividad sexual**
  Sexual activity
- ✓ **Manejando un automóvil**
  Driving car
- ✓ **Nadando**
  Swimming

¿El dolor de pecho empeora con el ejercicio / actividad?
Does the chest pain get worse with exertion/activity?

¿Ha tenido una lesión en el pecho recientemente?
Have you recently had a physical injury to your chest?

¿Le duele cuando presiono el pecho hacia abajo?
Does it hurt when I press down on your chest?

¿Le duele cuando respira?
Does it hurt when you breathe in?

¿El dolor del pecho lo hace sentir que le falta el aire?
Does your chest pain make you short of breath?

¿El dolor del pecho lo hace sentir náuseas?
Does your chest pain make you feel nauseated?

¿El dolor del pecho lo hace vomitar?
Does your chest pain make you vomit?

¿Siente un sudor frío cuando comienza
el dolor en el pecho?
Do you have a cold sweat when your chest pain begins?

¿Se pone pálido cuando le empieza el dolor?
Do you get pale when your chest pain begins?

¿Ha tenido un ataque al corazón en el pasado?
Have you had a heart attack?

¿Le duele el pecho como la última vez que
tuvo un ataque al corazón?
Does your chest pain feel like the last time you had a heart attack?

¿Cómo describiría el dolor?

How would you describe your chest pain?

Que duele
Aching

Abrazador
Burning

Con espasmos
Cramping

Devastador
Crushing

Que incomoda
Discomfort

Sordo
Dull

Que produce pesadez
Heaviness

Que produce picazón
Itching

En oleadas punzantes
Jabbing

Persistente
Nagging

Que acalambra
Numbness

Penetrante
Penetrating

Con palpitaciones
Pounding

Que ocasiona presión
Pressure

Que desgarra
Ripping

Que irradia
Radiating

Agudo
Sharp

Fulgurante
Shooting

Que resiente
Sore

Que causa espasmos
Spasms

Que aprieta
Squeezing

Lacerante
Stabbing

Que desgarra
Tearing

Sensible
Tender

Palpitante
Throbbing

Que oprime
Tightness

Que cansa
Tiring

No puedo describirlo.
I can't describe it.

CARDIOLOGY

30

¿El dolor irradia o se traslada a otra área de su cuerpo?
Does the pain radiate or move to another area of your body?

Si el dolor se irradia, por favor señale sobre su propio cuerpo donde se traslada.
If the pain radiates, please point on your own body where it goes.

Por favor, indique (en la siguiente escala) la intensidad de su dolor.
Please point (on this scale) to rate your pain.

| No hay dolor | Dolor moderado | Dolor intenso |

0   1   2   3   4   5   6   7   8   9   10

¿El dolor es constante o intermitente?
Is the pain constant or does it come and go?

  Constante
Constant

 Intermitente
Comes and goes

¿Ha tomado usted nitroglicerina hoy?
Have you taken nitroglycerin today?

¿La nitroglicerina le disminuye el dolor en el pecho?
Did the nitroglycerin improve your chest pain?

¿Ha tomado aspirina hoy?
Have you taken any aspirin today?

¿Ha tomado Viagra, Levitra o Cialis (medicamentos para la disfunción eréctil) durante las últimas 24 horas?
Have you taken Viagra, Levitra, or Cialis (medications for erectile dysfunction) within the last 24 hours?

¿Con cuántas almohadas duerme en la noche?
How many pillows do you sleep on at night?

0   1   2   3   4   5   >

¿Ese es el número de almohadas normal para usted?
Is this number of pillows normal for you?

¿Usted se despierta en la noche y tiene que sentarse o abrir la ventana para recuperar el aire?
Do you wake up at night and have to sit up or open the window to catch your breath?

¿Tiene tos?
Do you have a cough?

¿Tiene hinchazón en las piernas?
Do you have leg swelling?

¿Esta hinchazón en las piernas es algo nuevo?
Is this leg swelling new?

CARDIOLOGY

32

CARDIAC PROCEDURAL

Le voy a dar algo de oxígeno mediante el uso de una máscara que va en la cara o dentro la nariz. Puede ser incómodo.

I am going to give you some oxygen either by a mask that goes over you face or up your nose. It may be uncomfortable.

¿El oxígeno le está ayudando con el dolor en el pecho y/o la dificultad para respirar?

Is the oxygen helping your chest pain and/or shortness of breath?

Aquí tiene aspirina masticable. Por favor, mastíquela y tráguesela.

Here is some chewable aspirin. Please chew it up and swallow.

Le voy a administrar nitroglicerina. Por favor abra la boca y coloque la lengua en el paladar. Le voy a rociar el medicamento debajo de la lengua o le voy a colocar una pequeña tableta debajo de la lengua. Esto podría ocasionarle dolor de cabeza.

I am going to give you some nitroglycerin. Please open your mouth and put your tongue to the roof of your mouth. I will either spray some medicine under your tongue or place a small medicine tablet under your tongue. This may give you a headache.

Voy a colocarle unos adhesivos en los brazos y/o el tórax para medir la actividad eléctrica del corazón. Por favor, no se mueva. Esto no le va a doler.

I am going to put some stickers on your arms and/or chest to measure the electrical activity of your heart. Please stay very still. This will not hurt.

Voy a colocarle suero. Va a sentir una punzada brevemente pero esto es importante hacerlo para poder administrarle medicamentos.

I am going to start an IV. This may sting briefly, but is important so we can give you medication.

Tengo que utilizar una jeringa para obtener una muestra de sangre. Tal vez le arda brevemente pero esto es importante hacerlo para nosotros entender mejor cómo ayudarlo.

I need to use a needle to get a blood sample. This may sting briefly, but is important so we can better understand how to help you.

Le voy a administrar medicamento en el suero.

I am going to give you medication through your IV.

¿Cómo describiría en este momento el dolor en el pecho?

How would you now describe your chest pain?

 Mejor
Better

 Lo mismo
Same

 Peor
Worse

 Se me quitó
Gone

¿Ha cambiado de característica el dolor que siente en el pecho?

Has the quality of your chest pain changed?

CARDIOLOGY

34

PAST CARDIAC HISTORY

¿Usted tiene la presión sanguínea alta?
Do you have high blood pressure?

¿Tiene diabetes?
Do you have diabetes?

¿Ha tenido un infarto?
Have you had a heart attack?

¿Cuántos infartos ha tenido?
How many heart attacks have you had?

0   1   2   3   4   5   >

¿Le han colocado stents (prótesis endovascular)?
Have you had stents placed?

¿Alguna vez ha tomado medicamentos destructores de coágulos?
Have you ever received clot-busting drugs?

¿Ha tenido una embolia pulmonar?
Have you had a pulmonary embolism?

¿Ha tenido una trombosis venosa profunda?
Have you had a deep vein thrombosis?

¿Usted toma aspirina diariamente?
Do you take aspirin on a daily basis?

¿Usa usted diluyentes de la sangre?
Are you on blood thinners?

¿Le han realizado una cirugía de derivación coronaria?
Have you had a heart bypass surgery?

¿Usted sufre de vasos sanguíneos en mal estado?
Do you have bad blood vessels?

¿Ha tenido un aneurisma?
Have you had an aneurysm?

¿Tiene implantado un marcapasos o desfibrilador?
Do you have an implanted pacemaker/defibrillator?

¿Tiene historial de fibrilación auricular?
Do you have a history of atrial fibrillation?

¿Tiene historial de edema pulmonar?
Do you have a history of pulmonary edema?

¿Tiene historial de enfermedad pulmonar
obstructiva crónica?
Do you have a history of chronic obstructive pulmonary disease (COPD)?

¿Tiene historial de enfisema?
Do you have a history of emphysema?

¿Tiene historial de bronquitis?
Do you have a history of bronchitis?

ENDOCRINOLOGY

36

ACUTE ENDOCRINE HISTORY

¿Tiene diabetes?
Do you have diabetes?

¿Cuándo fue la última vez que se revisó el nivel de azúcar en la sangre?
When was the last time you checked your blood sugar level?

DÍAS DAYS	1	2	3	4	5	6	7		>
SEMANAS WEEKS	1	2	3	4	5	6	7	8	9	10	>
MESES MONTHS	1	2	3	4	5	6	7	8	9	10	>
AÑOS YEARS	1	2	3	4	5	6	7	8	9	10	>

¿Cuál era su nivel de azúcar en la sangre la última vez que se la revisó?
What was your blood sugar level when you checked it last?

Bajo — Alto

60   120   150   200   300

¿Se aplica insulina?
Do you take insulin?

 Sí
Yes

 No
No

 Ya no me aplico.
Not any more.

¿Cuándo se aplica normalmente la insulina?
When do you normally take your insulin?

EN LA MAÑANA	AL MEDIODÍA	CON LA CENA	EN LA NOCHE
MORNING	NOON	DINNER	NIGHT

¿Cuándo fue la última vez que se aplicó insulina?
When was the last time you took your insulin?

DÍAS DAYS	1	2	3	4	5	6	7 >			
SEMANAS WEEKS	1	2	3	4	5	6	7	8	9	10 >
MESES MONTHS	1	2	3	4	5	6	7	8	9	10 >

ENDOCRINE PROCEDURAL

Le voy a revisar el nivel de azúcar en la sangre. Va a sentir un pinchazo brevemente.

I am going to check your blood sugar. This might sting briefly.

Le voy a hacer una prueba de tolerancia a la glucosa. Va a sentir un pinchazo brevemente. Después que se tome el líquido revisaremos periódicamente sus niveles de azúcar en la sangre.

I am going to give you glucose tolerance test. This may sting briefly.
After drinking this liquid we will test your blood sugar levels periodically.

ENDOCRINOLOGY

38

Por favor, coma para que aumenten los niveles de azúcar en sangre.

Please eat so we can increase your blood sugar levels.

Le voy a administrar glucagon.

I am going to give you some glucagon.

Le voy a administrar insulina.

I am going to give you some insulin.

PAST ENDOCRINE HISTORY

¿Tiene diabetes tipo 1 o tipo 2?

Do you have Type 1 or Type 2 Diabetes?

¿Su nivel de azúcar en la sangre normalmente pasa de más de 120 [mg/dl]?

Does your blood sugar level typically run over 120 [mg/dl]?

¿Su nivel de azúcar en la sangre normalmente pasa de menos de 60 [mg/dl]?

Does your blood sugar level typically run under 60 [mg/dl]?

¿Usted toma medicamentos para la diabetes vía oral?

Do you take oral medication for your diabetes?

¿Alguna vez ha sido hospitalizado por tener niveles muy altos de azúcar en la sangre?

Have you ever been hospitalized for having very high blood sugar levels?

¿Alguna vez ha sido hospitalizado por tener niveles muy bajos de azúcar en la sangre?

Have you ever been hospitalized for having very low blood sugar levels?

Hola, soy un(a) profesional de la salud. No hablo español.

Hello, I am a healthcare professional. I do not speak Spanish.

Respóndame solo sí o no .

Only respond to me "yes" or "no."

ACUTE GASTROINTESTINAL HISTORY

¿Tiene dolor en la boca?
Do you have pain in your mouth?

¿Siente dolor al tragar?
Do you have pain when you swallow?

¿Tiene alguna lesión en la boca?
Do you have any lesions in your mouth?

¿Siente acidez estomacal sin haber comido alimentos?
Do you have heartburn without food?

¿Siente acidez estomacal sin haber comido?
Do you have heartburn without eating?

¿Siente náuseas?
Are you nauseated?

¿Cuántas veces siente náuseas durante el día?
How often are you nauseated during a day?

Rara vez	A veces	A menudo	Siempre

GASTROINTESTINAL

40

¿Siente náuseas antes o después de comer?
Does the nausea come before or after eating?

✓ **Antes de comer**
Before eating

✓ **Después de comer**
After eating

✓ **Ambos**
Both

✓ **En ninguno de los casos**
Neither

✓ **No lo sé.**
I don't know.

¿Usted vomita con regularidad?
Do you vomit regularly?

¿Cuánto a menudo vomita?
How often do you vomit?

HORAS   2   4   6   8   10   12   14   16   18   20   22   >
Hours

¿De qué color es el vómito?
What color is the vomit?

✓ **Negro**
Black

✓ **Rojo intenso**
Bright red

✓ **Transparente**
Clear

✓ **Rojo oscuro**
Dark red

✓ **Verde**
Green

✓ **Mucoso**
Mucousy

✓ **Rojo**
Red

✓ **Marrón claro**
Tan

✓ **Alimento no digerido**
Undigested food

✓ **Amarillo**
Yellow

GASTROINTESTINAL

¿Hay sangre en el vómito?
Is there blood in the vomit?

¿Qué tanta cantidad de sangre hay en el vómito?
How much blood is in the vomit?

Ninguna	Un poco	La mitad	Mucho	Sólo sangre

¿Vomita antes o después de comer?
Does the vomit come before or after eating?

 Antes
Before

 En ninguno de los casos
Neither

 Después
After

 No lo sé.
I don't know.

 Ambos
Both

¿Puede usted tragar y retener los líquidos?
Can you swallow and and keep down liquids?

¿Puede usted tragar y retener los sólidos?
Can you swallow and keep down solids?

¿Siente dolor en el estómago?
Do you have abdominal pain?

Por favor, señale sobre su propio abdomen exactamente donde siente dolor.
Please point on your own abdomen exactly where you have abdominal pain.

GASTROINTESTINAL

42

¿Cuándo comenzó el dolor?
When did your pain begin?

MINUTOS Minutes	10	20	30	40	50	60					
HORAS Hours	2	4	6	8	10	12	14	16	18	20	22
DÍAS Days	1	2	3	4	5	6	7	8	9	10	>
SEMANAS Weeks	1	2	3	4	5	6	7	8	9	10	>
MESES Months	1	2	3	4	5	6	7	8	9	10	>
AÑOS Years	1	2	3	4	5	6	7	8	9	10	>

¿Cómo describiría el inicio del dolor?
How would you describe the onset of your pain?

 Lo despertó después de estar dormido
Awakened from sleep

 Gradual
Gradual

 Continuo
Ongoing

 Progresivo
Progressive

 Repentino
Sudden

 No lo sé.
I don't know.

¿El dolor empeora al comer?
Does the pain get worse with eating?

¿El dolor disminuye al comer?
Does the pain get better with eating?

¿El dolor empeora al moverse?
Does the pain get worse when moving?

¿El dolor empeora al quedarse quieto?
Does the pain get worse when staying still?

¿Qué hace que el dolor disminuya?
What makes the pain better?

 Al moverse
Moving

 El hielo/el frío
Ice/cold

 Al posicionarse
Adjusting your position

 El calor
Heat

 Medicamentos
Medication

 La actividad
Physical activity

¿Qué hace que el dolor empeore?
What makes the pain worse?

 Al estar parado
Standing

 Al respirar
Breathing

 Al tocarse o que lo toquen
Touch

 Al comer
Eating

 Al orinar
Urination

Al moverse
Movement

 Al caminar
Walking

GASTROINTESTINAL

44

¿Cómo describiría el dolor?
How would you describe your pain?

- ✓ **Que duele**
  Aching

- ✓ **Abrazador**
  Burning

- ✓ **Con espasmos**
  Cramping

- ✓ **Devastador**
  Crushing

- ✓ **Que incomoda**
  Discomfort

- ✓ **Sordo**
  Dull

- ✓ **Que produce pesadez**
  Heaviness

- ✓ **Que produce picazón**
  Itching

- ✓ **En oleadas punzantes**
  Jabbing

- ✓ **Persistente**
  Nagging

- ✓ **Que acalambra**
  Numbness

- ✓ **Penetrante**
  Penetrating

- ✓ **Con palpitaciones**
  Pounding

- ✓ **Que ocasiona presión**
  Pressure

- ✓ **Que desgarra**
  Ripping

- ✓ **Que irradia**
  Radiating

- ✓ **Agudo**
  Sharp

- ✓ **Fulgurante**
  Shooting

- ✓ **Que resiente**
  Sore

- ✓ **Que causa espasmos**
  Spasms

- ✓ **Que aprieta**
  Squeezing

- ✓ **Lacerante**
  Stabbing

- ✓ **Que desgarra**
  Tearing

- ✓ **Sensible**
  Tender

- ✓ **Palpitante**
  Throbbing

- ✓ **Que oprime**
  Tightness

- ✓ **Que cansa**
  Tiring

- ✓ **No puedo describirlo.**
  I can't describe it.

¿El dolor irradia o se traslada a otra área de su cuerpo?
Does the pain radiate or move to another area of your body?

Si el dolor se irradia, por favor señale sobre su propio cuerpo donde se traslada.
If the pain radiates, please point on your own body where it goes.

Por favor, indique (en la siguiente escala) la intensidad de su dolor.
Please point (on this scale) to rate your pain.

No hay dolor   Dolor moderado   Dolor intenso

0 1 2 3 4 5 6 7 8 9 10

¿El dolor es constante o intermitente?
Is the pain constant or does it come and go?

 Constante
Constant

 Intermitente
Comes and goes

¿Cuándo fue la última vez que defecó?
When was your last bowel movement?

DÍAS   1 2 3 4 5 6 7 8 9 10 >
Days

SEMANAS   1 2 3 4 5 6 7 8 9 10 >
Weeks

GASTROINTESTINAL

46

¿Ha perdido el control de los intestinos (incontinencia)?
Have you lost control of your bowels (incontinence)?

¿Tiene deposiciones normales?
Do you have normal bowel movements?

¿Cómo describiría su más reciente deposición?
How would you describe your most recent bowel movement?

 Negra
Black

 Roja
Red

 Marrón
Brown

 Con vetas rojas
Red streaks

 Arcilla
Clay

 Marrón clara
Tan

 Verde
Green

 Amarilla
Yellow

 Meconio
Meconium

 Blanca
White

¿De qué tamaño describiría su más reciente deposición?
How large was your most recent bowel movement?

Pequeña   Mediana   Grande

├─────────────────────────────┼─────────────────────────────┤

¿De dónde procede la más reciente deposición?
Where did your most recent bowel movement come from?

 De una colostomía
Colostomy

 De un sistema de manejo fecal
Fecal management system

 De una Ileostomía
Ileostomy

 Del recto
Rectum

 De una yeyunostomía
Jejunostomy

¿Había sangre presente en la materia fecal?
Did your stool have blood in it?

¿Tiene diarrea?
Do you have diarrhea?

¿Tiene estreñimiento?
Are you constipated?

¿Cuándo fue la última vez que hizo una deposición normal?
When was the last time you had a normal bowel movement?

DÍAS DAYS	1	2	3	4	5	6	7	8	9	10	>

SEMANAS WEEKS	1	2	3	4	5	6	7	8	9	10	>

¿Con qué frecuencia hace deposiciones?
How often are you moving your bowels?

1   2   3   4   5   6   7   >   **CADA DÍA**

GASTROINTESTINAL

48

¿Cómo describiría las heces fecales?
How would you describe your stool?

 Normales
Normal

 Suaves
Soft

Líquidas
Liquid

Anormales
Abnormal

Dolorosas
Painful

¿Siente ganas de defecar pero no puede?
Do you feel the urge to move your bowels but can't?

¿Tiene picazón?
Do you have itching?

¿Ha notado erupciones cutáneas en sus glúteos y recto?
Have you noticed rashes around your buttocks/rectum?

¿Qué medicamentos usa usted para cualquiera de estos problemas?
What medications have you taken for any of these problems?

 Crema tópica
Topical cream

Ungüento
Ointment

Medicamento vía oral
Oral medication

 Otros
Other

 Nada
Nothing

¿Los medicamentos le aliviaron el malestar?
Did the medications alleviate your discomfort?

GASTROINTESTINAL PROCEDURAL

Voy a presionar en varios lugares del abdomen para examinarlo.
Esto puede doler y/o ser incómodo.

I am going to press down in various places on your abdomen to examine it.
This may hurt and/or be uncomfortable.

Le voy a administrar medicamento para ablandar las heces fecales.

I am going to give you some medication to soften your stool.

Le voy a administrar líquidos en el suero.

I am going to give you fluids through your IV.

PAST GASTROINTESTINAL HISTORY

¿Ha tenido alguna cirugía abdominal?

Have you had abdominal surgery?

¿Usted padece de enfermedad de Crohn?

Do you have Crohn's Disease?

¿Tiene síndrome de intestino irritable?

Do you have Irritable Bowel Syndrome?

¿Alguna vez ha tenido una hernia?

Have you ever had a hernia?

¿Le han sacado?:   La vesícula   *Gall Bladder*

Have you had this removed:

El bazo   *Spleen*

El apéndice   *Appendix*

GASTROINTESTINAL

50

¿Tiene historial de?:

Do you have a history of:

Spanish			English
Colecistitis	✓	✗	*Cholecystitis*
Sangrado intestinal	✓	✗	*Intestinal bleeding*
Problemas de vesícula	✓	✗	*Gall bladder problems*
Cálculos biliares	✓	✗	*Gall stones*
Problemas de hígado	✓	✗	*Liver problems*
Hepatitis A	✓	✗	*Hepatitis A*
Hepatitis B	✓	✗	*Hepatitis B*
Hepatitis C	✓	✗	*Hepatitis C*
Cirrosis del hígado	✓	✗	*Cirrhosis of the liver*
Pancreatitis	✓	✗	*Pancreatitis*
Problemas del bazo	✓	✗	*Spleen problems*
Problemas de colitis ulcerosa	✓	✗	*Ulcerative colitis*
Problemas de obstrucción intestinal	✓	✗	*Bowel obstructions*
Sangrado en el intestino delgado	✓	✗	*Bleeding in small intestine*
Sangrado en el intestino grueso	✓	✗	*Bleeding in large intestine (colon)*
Problemas de riñones	✓	✗	*Kidney problems*

ACUTE GYNECOLOGICAL HISTORY

¿Tiene dolor en la pelvis?
Do you have pain in your pelvis?

Por favor, indique (en la siguiente escala) la intensidad de su dolor.
Please point (on this scale) to rate your pain.

| No hay dolor | Dolor moderado | Dolor intenso |

0   1   2   3   4   5   6   7   8   9   10

¿Cuándo comenzó el dolor?
When did your pain begin?

MINUTOS MINUTES	10	20	30	40	50	60					
HORAS HOURS	2	4	6	8	10	12	14	16	18	20	22
DÍAS DAYS	1	2	3	4	5	6	7	8	9	10	>
SEMANAS WEEKS	1	2	3	4	5	6	7	8	9	10	>
MESES MONTHS	1	2	3	4	5	6	7	8	9	10	>

GYNECOLOGY

¿Cómo describiría el inicio del dolor?
How would you describe the onset of your pain?

✓ **Lo despertó después de estar dormido**
Awakened from sleep

✓ **Gradual**
Gradual

✓ **Continuo**
Ongoing

✓ **Progresivo**
Progressive

✓ **Repentino**
Sudden

✓ **No lo sé.**
I don't know.

¿Qué hace que el dolor empeore?
What makes the pain worse?

✓ **Al respirar**
Breathing

✓ **Al comer**
Eating

✓ **Al moverse**
Movement

✓ **Al estar parado**
Standing

✓ **Al estar acostado**
Lying down

✓ **Al defecar**
Defecating

✓ **Al tocarse o que lo toquen**
Touch

✓ **Al orinar**
Urination

✓ **Al caminar**
Walking

✓ **Al toser**
Coughing

✓ **Al correr**
Running

✓ **Actividad sexual**
Sexual activity

¿Cómo describiría el dolor?
How would you describe your pain?

✓ **Que duele**
Aching

✓ **Abrazador**
Burning

✓ **Con espasmos**
Cramping

✓ **Devastador**
Crushing

✓ **Que incomoda**
Discomfort

✓ **Sordo**
Dull

✓ **Que produce pesadez**
Heaviness

✓ **Que produce picazón**
Itching

✓ **En oleadas punzantes**
Jabbing

✓ **Persistente**
Nagging

✓ **Que acalambra**
Numbness

✓ **Penetrante**
Penetrating

✓ **Con palpitaciones**
Pounding

✓ **Que ocasiona presión**
Pressure

✓ **Que desgarra**
Ripping

✓ **Que irradia**
Radiating

✓ **Agudo**
Sharp

✓ **Fulgurante**
Shooting

✓ **Que resiente**
Sore

✓ **Que causa espasmos**
Spasms

✓ **Que aprieta**
Squeezing

✓ **Lacerante**
Stabbing

✓ **Que desgarra**
Tearing

✓ **Sensible**
Tender

✓ **Palpitante**
Throbbing

✓ **Que oprime**
Tightness

✓ **Que cansa**
Tiring

✓ **No puedo describirlo.**
I can't describe it.

¿El dolor irradia o se traslada a otra área de su cuerpo?
Does the pain radiate or move to another area of your body?

Si el dolor se irradia, por favor señale sobre su propio cuerpo donde se traslada.
If the pain radiates, please point on your own body where it goes.

Por favor, indique (en la siguiente escala) la intensidad de su dolor.
Please point (on this scale) to rate your pain.

No hay dolor   Dolor moderado   Dolor intenso

0   1   2   3   4   5   6   7   8   9   10

¿El dolor es constante o intermitente?
Is the pain constant or does it come and go?

 Constante
Constant

 Intermitente
Comes and goes

¿Tiene sangrado vaginal anormal?
Do you have abnormal vaginal bleeding?

¿Este sangrado ocurre durante su período normal o no ocurre durante su período?
Does this bleeding occur during your normal period or not during your period?

¿Cuántas toallas sanitarias ha usado desde que comenzó a sangrar?
How many pads have you gone through since your bleeding started?

0   1   2   3   4   5   >

¿El sangrado es doloroso?
Is the bleeding painful?

¿Tiene secreción vaginal anormal?
Do you have an abnormal vaginal discharge?

¿De qué color es?
What color is it?

 Negra
Black

 Roja
Red

 Marrón
Brown

 Amarilla
Yellow

 Verde
Green

¿Tiene mal olor la secreción vaginal?
Does the abnormal vaginal discharge smell bad?

¿Cómo describiría la secreción vaginal anormal?
How would you describe the abnormal vaginal discharge?

 Líquida
Liquid

 Pegajosa
Sticky

 Mucosa
Mucus-like

 Sólida
Solid

GYNECOLOGY

56

GYNECOLOGY PROCEDURAL

Por favor, cámbiese de ropa y póngase esta bata.

Please change out of your clothes and into this gown.

Por favor, acuéstese en la mesa y ponga los pies en los estribos.

Please lie down on the table and put your feet into the stirrups.

Voy a colocarle este espéculo en la vagina para examinarla.

Primero va a sentir que la toco y después va a sentir el espéculo.

Esto puede ser un poco incómodo.

I am going to place this speculum into your vagina to examine it.

First you will feel my touch, then you will feel the speculum.

This may be uncomfortable.

Voy a recoger una muestra del interior de la vagina.

Esto puede ser un poco incómodo.

I am going to swab the inside of your vagina and take a sample.

This may be uncomfortable.

Por favor, relájese.

Please relax.

Hemos terminado.

We are done.

Por favor, póngase su ropa.

Please change back into your own clothes.

PAST GYNECOLOGICAL HISTORY

¿Ya empezó su ciclo menstrual?
Have you started your menstrual cycle yet?

¿Su período/ciclo menstrual es regular?
Is your period/menstrual cycle regular?

Indique cuántas semanas han pasado desde la última menstruación.
Indicate how many weeks have passed since your last menstrual period.

SEMANAS WEEKS	1	2	3	4	5	6	7	8	9	10	>
MESES MONTHS	1	2	3	4	5	6	7	8	9	10	>
AÑOS YEARS	1	2	3	4	5	6	7	8	9	10	>

¿Qué edad tenía cuando tuvo su primer período?
How old were you when you had your first period?

10   **11**   **12**   **13**   **14**   **15**   **16**   **17**   **18**   **>**

¿Cuánto le dura el período normal?
How long does your normal period last?

DÍAS DAYS	1	2	3	4	5	6	7	8	9	10	>

¿Cómo describiría normalmente el color de la sangre del período?
How would you normally describe the color of your period blood?

Rojo claro   Rojo   Oscuro

¿Cuántas toallas sanitarias o tampones usa normalmente durante su período?
How many pads, sanitary napkins, or tampons do you normally go through during your period?

0   1   2   3   4   5   6   7   8   9   10   >

¿Normalmente tiene cólicos durante su período?
Do you normally have cramps during your period?

Por favor, indique (en la siguiente escala) la intensidad de su dolor.
Please point (on this scale) to rate your pain.

No hay dolor   Dolor moderado   Dolor intenso

0 1 2 3 4 5 6 7 8 9 10

¿Ha estado embarazada alguna vez?
Have you ever been pregnant?

Indique el número de veces que ha estado embarazada.
Indicate how many times you have been pregnant.

1   2   3   4   5   6   7   8   9   10   >

¿Tiene hijos?
Do you have any children?

Indique el número de hijos que tiene.
Indicate how many children you have.

1   2   3   4   5   6   7   8   9   10   >

¿Alguna vez le han practicado un aborto o ha tenido un aborto espontaneo?
Have you ever had an abortion or a miscarriage?

Indique el número de abortos provocados o abortos espontáneos que haya tenido.
Indicate how many abortions or miscarriages you have had.

1   2   3   4   5   6   7   8   9   10   >

¿Alguna vez ha tenido un embarazo ectópico anterior?
Have you ever had a previous ectopic pregnancy?

¿Ha tenido complicaciones con un embarazo anterior?
Have you had complications with a past pregnancy?

¿Cómo describiría su actividad sexual?

How would best describe your sexual activity?

 Inactiva
Inactive

 No muy activa
Not very active

Moderada
Moderate

Activa
Active

Frecuente
Frequent

¿Cuántos compañeros sexuales ha tenido?

How many sexual partners have you had?

1 2 3 4 5 6 7 8 9 10 >

¿Tiene relaciones sexuales con hombres, mujeres, o con ambos?

Do you have sex with men, women, or both?

 Hombre
Male

 Mujer
Female

 Ambos
Both

¿Usa anticonceptivos?

Do you use contraception?

 Sí
Yes

No
No

Sí, a veces
Sometimes

¿Alguna vez ha tenido relaciones sexuales sin protección?

Have you ever had unprotected sex?

¿Cuándo fue la última vez que tuvo relaciones sexuales sin protección?
When was the last time you had unprotected sex?

HORAS	2	4	6	8	10	12	14	16	18	20	22
HOURS											

DÍAS	1	2	3	4	5	6	7	8	9	10	>
DAYS											

SEMANAS	1	2	3	4	5	6	7	8	9	10	>
WEEKS											

MESES	1	2	3	4	5	6	7	8	9	10	>
MONTHS											

¿Alguna vez ha contraído una enfermedad de transmisión sexual?

Have you ever contracted a sexually transmitted diseased?

¿Alguna vez ha sido víctima de violencia?

Have you ever been a victim of violence?

¿Ha sido víctima de violencia en los últimos 6 meses?

Have you been a victim of violence within the past 6 months?

¿Alguien la ha obligado a tener relaciones sexuales sin su consentimiento?

Has anyone ever forced you into sexual activity unwillingly?

¿Las relaciones sexuales sin su consentimiento ocurrieron en los últimos 6 meses?

Did the unwanted sexual activity occur within the past 6 months?

NEUROLOGY

62

ACUTE NEUROLOGICAL HISTORY

¿Los síntomas comenzaron hoy?
Did your symptoms begin today?

Si los síntomas empezaron hoy, por favor indique cuando empezaron.
If the symptoms began today please indicate when they began.

AM	1	2	3	4	5	6	7	8	9	10	11	12
PM	1	2	3	4	5	6	7	8	9	10	11	12

Si los síntomas empezaron antes del día de hoy, por favor
indique cuando empezaron.
If the symptoms began before today please indicate when they began.

DÍAS DAYS	1	2	3	4	5	6	7	8	9	10	>
SEMANAS WEEKS	1	2	3	4	5	6	7	8	9	10	>
MESES MONTHS	1	2	3	4	5	6	7	8	9	10	>
AÑOS YEARS	1	2	3	4	5	6	7	8	9	10	>

FOR CAREGIVER/FAMILY/WITNESS

Por favor, indique cuándo aproximadamente se encontró al paciente.
Please indicate approximately when the patient was found.

AM	1	2	3	4	5	6	7	8	9	10	11	12
PM	1	2	3	4	5	6	7	8	9	10	11	12

¿Cuándo fue la última vez que al paciente se le vio normal?
When was the last time the patient seemed normal?

MINUTOS MINUTES	10	20	30	40	50	60					
HORAS HOURS	2	4	6	8	10	12	14	16	18	20	22
DÍAS DAYS	1	2	3	4	5	6	7	8	9	10	>
SEMANAS WEEKS	1	2	3	4	5	6	7	8	9	10	>
MESES MONTHS	1	2	3	4	5	6	7	8	9	10	>
AÑOS YEARS	1	2	3	4	5	6	7	8	9	10	>

BACK TO PATIENT

¿Tiene desmayos?
Are you having blackout spells?

¿Ha tenido desmayos en el pasado?
Have you had blackouts in the past?

¿Cuánto tiempo ha tenido desmayos?
How long have you had blackouts?

SEMANAS / Weeks	1	2	3	4	5	6	7	8	9	10	>
MESES / Months	1	2	3	4	5	6	7	8	9	10	>
AÑOS / Years	1	2	3	4	5	6	7	8	9	10	>

¿Con qué frecuencia se desmaya?
How often do you have blackouts?

 Diariamente
Daily

1-5 por mes
1-5 per month

 1-5 por semana
1-5 per week

 1-5 por año
1-5 per year

¿Cuánto tiempo duran los desmayos?
How long do the blackouts last?

30 SEC | **1 MIN** | **5 MIN** | **15 MIN** | **30 MIN** | **1 HR** | **6 HR**

NEUROLOGY

¿Puede anticipar cuando está a punto de desmayarse?
Can you tell when you are about to have a blackout?

¿Recuerda que se desmayó?
Do you remember having the blackout?

¿Los desmayos hacen que se contorsione o sacuda?
Do the blackouts cause you to twitch or jerk?

¿Los desmayos hacen que pierda el control de
la vejiga o los intestinos?
Do the blackouts cause you to lose control of your bladder or bowels?

¿Los desmayos hacen que se muerda la lengua o la mejilla?
Do the blackouts cause you to bite your tongue or cheek?

¿Después de los desmayos se siente confundido
o desorientado?
After the blackouts do you feel confused or disoriented?

¿Después de los desmayos se siente cansado?
After the blackouts do you feel tired?

¿Después de los desmayos se siente enojado o irritado?
After the blackouts do you feel angry or upset?

¿Es usted capaz de controlar los intestinos y/o la vejiga?
Are you able to control your bowels and/or bladder?

¿La pérdida de control de los intestinos y/o de la
vejiga ocurre de repente?
Did the loss of control of your bowels and/or bladder occur suddenly?

NEUROLOGY

¿Ha tenido problemas de confusión o pérdida de la memoria?

Have you had any problems with confusion or loss of memory?

¿Cuándo comenzó la confusión o pérdida de la memoria?

When did the confusion or memory loss start?

MINUTOS MINUTES	10	20	30	40	50	60					
HORAS HOURS	2	4	6	8	10	12	14	16	18	20	22
DÍAS DAYS	1	2	3	4	5	6	7	8	9	10	>
SEMANAS WEEKS	1	2	3	4	5	6	7	8	9	10	>
MESES MONTHS	1	2	3	4	5	6	7	8	9	10	>
AÑOS YEARS	1	2	3	4	5	6	7	8	9	10	>

¿La confusión o pérdida de la memoria es constante o intermitente?

Is the confusion or memory loss constant or does it come and go?

 Constante
Constant

 Intermitente
Comes and goes

¿Tiene mareos o problemas de equilibrio?
Do you have dizziness or balance problems?

¿Ha tenido problemas de mareos o de equilibrio?
Have you had dizziness/balance problems in the past?

¿Tiene problemas de mareos o de equilibrio en la cabeza o en las piernas?
Do you have dizziness/balance problems in the head or in the legs?

 En la cabeza
Head

 Con ambos
Both

 En las piernas
Legs

 No
No

¿Cuándo comenzaron los problemas de mareo o de equilibrio?
When did the dizziness/balance problems start?

MINUTOS MINUTES	10	20	30	40	50	60					
HORAS HOURS	2	4	6	8	10	12	14	16	18	20	22
DÍAS DAYS	1	2	3	4	5	6	7	8	9	10	>
SEMANAS WEEKS	1	2	3	4	5	6	7	8	9	10	>
MESES MONTHS	1	2	3	4	5	6	7	8	9	10	>
AÑOS YEARS	1	2	3	4	5	6	7	8	9	10	>

NEUROLOGY

68

¿Con qué frecuencia se siente mareado/desequilibrado?
How often do you feel dizzy/off balance?

- ✓ **Diariamente**
  Daily

- ✓ **1-5 por semana**
  1-5 per week

- ✓ **1-5 por mes**
  1-5 per month

- ✓ **1-5 por año**
  1-5 per year

¿Cuánto tiempo dura el mareo/problema de equilibrio?
How long does the dizziness/balance problem last?

30 SEC | **1 MIN** | **15 MIN** | **30 MIN** | **1 HR** | **6 HR** | **12 HR** >

¿Describiría sus mareos como una sensación en que todo da vueltas, aturdimiento o pérdida del equilibrio?
Would you describe your dizziness as a spinning, lightheaded, or off balance feeling?

- ✓ **Mareos**
  Dizziness

- ✓ **Aturdimiento**
  Lightheadedness

- ✓ **Ambas cosas**
  Both

- ✗ **No**
  No

¿El mareo empeora cuando se acuesta o se da vuelta?
Does the dizziness get worse when you lie down or roll over?   ✓ ✗

¿El mareo empeora cuando se para o camina?
Does the dizziness get worse when you stand up or walk?   ✓ ✗

¿Siente náuseas?
Do you feel nauseous?

¿Ha estado vomitando?
Have you been vomiting?

¿Ha estado sudando?
Have you been sweating?

¿Ha tenido pérdida de la audición últimamente?
Do you have recent hearing loss?

¿Siente dolor de oído?
Do you have ear pain?

¿Tiene palpitaciones?
Do you have palpitations?

¿Usted toma medicamentos para el mareo?
Do you take any medications for your dizziness?

¿Tiene dolor de cabeza?
Do you have a headache?

Por favor, señale en su propia cabeza donde siente los dolores de cabeza.
Please point to the location on your own head where the headaches are.

¿El dolor se traslada?
Does the pain move?

Por favor, señale en su propia cabeza hacia donde se desplaza el dolor.
Please point to the location on your own head where the pain moves.

NEUROLOGY

70

¿Ha tenido dolores de cabeza en el pasado?
Have you had headaches in the past?

¿Este dolor de cabeza es diferente o igual a los anteriores
dolores de cabeza?
Is this headache different or the same as your prior headaches?

 Igual
Same

 Diferente
Different

¿Cuándo comenzaron los dolores de cabeza?
When did the headaches start?

MINUTOS MINUTES	10	20	30	40	50	60					
HORAS HOURS	2	4	6	8	10	12	14	16	18	20	22
DÍAS DAYS	1	2	3	4	5	6	7	8	9	10	>
SEMANAS WEEKS	1	2	3	4	5	6	7	8	9	10	>
MESES MONTHS	1	2	3	4	5	6	7	8	9	10	>
AÑOS YEARS	1	2	3	4	5	6	7	8	9	10	>

¿Con qué frecuencia le dan dolores de cabeza?
How often do you get headaches?

- **Nunca antes**
  Never before

- **Diariamente**
  Daily

- **1-5 por semana**
  1-5 per week

- **1-5 por mes**
  1-5 per month

- **1-5 por año**
  1-5 per year

¿Cuánto tiempo duran los dolores de cabeza?
How long do your headaches last?

30 SEC | **1 MIN** | **15 MIN** | **30 MIN** | **1 HR** | **6 HR** | **12 HR** >

¿Cómo describiría los dolores de cabeza?
How would you describe your headaches?

- **Palpitante**
  Throbbing

- **Presión/dolor sordo**
  Pressure/dull

- **Lacerante**
  Stabbing

- **Otro**
  Other

Por favor, indique (en la siguiente escala) la intensidad de su dolor.
Please point (on this scale) to rate your pain.

No hay dolor — Dolor moderado — Dolor intenso

0 1 2 3 4 5 6 7 8 9 10

NEUROLOGY

72

¿Los dolores de cabeza están asociados con?:
Are your headaches associated with:

Sensibilidad a la luz		*Light sensitivity*
Sensibilidad al sonido		*Sound sensitivity*
Náuseas y vomito		*Nausea and vomiting*
Visión borrosa o puntos negros en la visión		*Blurred vision or black spots*
Un tipo particular de comida		*Specific foods*

¿Usted toma medicamentos para el dolor de cabeza?
Do you take any medications for your headaches?

Si usted tiene sus medicamentos aquí, por favor muéstremelos.
If you have your medications with you, please show them to me.

¿Usted tomó sus medicamentos hoy?
Did you take your medications today?

¿Siente rigidez en el cuello desde que el dolor comenzó?
Does your neck feel stiff since the headaches began?

¿Ha tenido usted fiebre o infección recientemente?
Have you had a recent fever or infection?

¿Tiene dolor de cuello o de espalda?
Do you have neck or back pain?

Sírvase indicar cuándo comenzó el dolor.
Please indicate when your pain began.

| **MINUTOS** | 10 | 20 | 30 | 40 | 50 | 60 | | | | |
| MINUTES | | | | | | | | | | |

| **HORAS** | 2 | 4 | 6 | 8 | 10 | 12 | 14 | 16 | 18 | 20 | 22 |
| HOURS | | | | | | | | | | | |

| **DÍAS** | 1 | 2 | 3 | 4 | 5 | 6 | 7 | 8 | 9 | 10 | > |
| DAYS | | | | | | | | | | | |

| **SEMANAS** | 1 | 2 | 3 | 4 | 5 | 6 | 7 | 8 | 9 | 10 | > |
| WEEKS | | | | | | | | | | | |

| **MESES** | 1 | 2 | 3 | 4 | 5 | 6 | 7 | 8 | 9 | 10 | > |
| MONTHS | | | | | | | | | | | |

| **AÑOS** | 1 | 2 | 3 | 4 | 5 | 6 | 7 | 8 | 9 | 10 | > |
| YEARS | | | | | | | | | | | |

¿El dolor del cuello o la espalda es constante o intermitente?
Is your neck or back pain constant or does it come and go?

 Constante
Constant

 Intermitente
Comes and goes

¿Cómo describiría el dolor?
How would you describe your neck or back pain?

 Sordo
Dull

 Agudo
Sharp

 Como descarga eléctrica
Electric Shock

 Lacerante
Stabbing

NEUROLOGY

74

¿Se lesionó el cuello o la espalda?
Did you injure your neck or back?

¿El dolor se irradia desde el cuello hasta el brazo?
Does the pain radiate from the neck into your arm?

¿El dolor se irradia desde la espalda hasta la pierna?
Does the pain radiate from your back into your leg?

¿Tiene entumecimiento?
Do you have numbness?

Por favor, señale en su propio cuerpo donde tiene entumecimiento.
Please point on your own body to where you are numb.

¿Siente entumecimiento en el lado izquierdo de su cuerpo,
en el lado derecho o ambos?
Do you feel numbness on the left side of your body, right side
of your body, or both?

 Izquierdo
Left

 Derecho
Right

En ambos
Both

¿Siente entumecimiento en la cara, los brazos, las piernas o los tres?
Do you feel numbness in the face, arms, legs, or all three?

 En la cara
Face

 En las piernas
Legs

En los brazos
Arms

 Los tres
All three

¿Cuándo comenzó el entumecimiento?
When did the numbness start?

| **MINUTOS** | 10 | 20 | 30 | 40 | 50 | 60 | | | | | |
| MINUTES | | | | | | | | | | | |

| **HORAS** | 2 | 4 | 6 | 8 | 10 | 12 | 14 | 16 | 18 | 20 | 22 |
| HOURS | | | | | | | | | | | |

| **DÍAS** | 1 | 2 | 3 | 4 | 5 | 6 | 7 | 8 | 9 | 10 | > |
| DAYS | | | | | | | | | | | |

| **SEMANAS** | 1 | 2 | 3 | 4 | 5 | 6 | 7 | 8 | 9 | 10 | > |
| WEEKS | | | | | | | | | | | |

| **MESES** | 1 | 2 | 3 | 4 | 5 | 6 | 7 | 8 | 9 | 10 | > |
| MONTHS | | | | | | | | | | | |

| **AÑOS** | 1 | 2 | 3 | 4 | 5 | 6 | 7 | 8 | 9 | 10 | > |
| YEARS | | | | | | | | | | | |

¿El entumecimiento inicio de repente?
Did the numbness start suddenly?

¿El entumecimiento es constante o intermitente?
Is the numbness constant or does it come and go?

 Constante
Constant

 Intermitente
Comes and goes

¿Tiene ataques convulsivos?
Do you have seizures?

¿Ha tenido ataques convulsivos en el pasado?
Have you had seizures in the past?

NEUROLOGY

76

¿Cuándo fue la última vez que tuvo un ataque?
When was your last seizure?

MINUTOS MINUTES	10	20	30	40	50	60					
HORAS HOURS	2	4	6	8	10	12	14	16	18	20	22
DÍAS DAYS	1	2	3	4	5	6	7	8	9	10	>
SEMANAS WEEKS	1	2	3	4	5	6	7	8	9	10	>
MESES MONTHS	1	2	3	4	5	6	7	8	9	10	>
AÑOS YEARS	1	2	3	4	5	6	7	8	9	10	>

¿Cuánto tiempo hace que tiene ataques?
How long have you had seizures?

SEMANAS WEEKS	1	2	3	4	5	6	7	8	9	10	>
MESES MONTHS	1	2	3	4	5	6	7	8	9	10	>
AÑOS YEARS	1	2	3	4	5	6	7	8	9	10	>

¿Con qué frecuencia tiene ataques?
How often do you have seizures?

✓ **Diariamente**
Daily

✓ **1-5 por mes**
1-5 per month

✓ **1-5 por semana**
1-5 per week

✓ **1-5 por año**
1-5 per year

¿Cuánto tiempo duran los ataques?
How long do the seizures last?

30 SEC | **1 MIN** | **15 MIN** | **30 MIN** | **1 HR** | **6 HR** | **12 HR** >

¿Puede anticipar cuando está a punto de tener un ataque?
Can you tell when you are about to have a seizure?

¿Recuerda después que tuvo un ataque?
Do you remember having the seizures?

¿Los ataques hacen que se contorsione o sacuda?
Do the seizures cause you to twitch or jerk?

¿Los ataques hacen que pierda el control de la vejiga o los intestinos?
Do the seizures cause you to lose control of your bladder or bowels?

¿Los ataques hacen que se muerda la lengua o la mejilla?
Do the seizures cause you to bite your tongue or cheek?

¿Después de los ataques se siente confundido o desorientado?
After the seizures do you feel confused or disoriented?

NEUROLOGY

78

¿Después de los ataques se siente cansado?
After the seizures do you feel tired?

¿Después de los ataques se siente enojado o irritado?
After the seizures do you feel angry or upset?

¿Usted toma medicamentos para los ataques?
Do you take medication for your seizures?

¿Tiene dificultades para hablar?
Are you having difficulty speaking?

¿Los problemas del habla comenzaron de repente?
Did the speech problems begin suddenly?

¿Tiene dificultades al tragar?
Do you have difficulty swallowing?

¿Los problemas al tragar comenzaron de repente?
Did the difficulty swallowing begin suddenly?

¿Tiene debilidad?
Do you have weakness?

Por favor, señale en su propio cuerpo donde tiene debilidad.
Please point on your own body where you have weakness.

¿Siente debilidad en el lado izquierdo de su cuerpo, en el lado derecho o ambos?
Do you feel weakness on the left side of your body, right side of your body, or both?

 Izquierdo
Left

 Derecho
Right

 En ambos
Both

¿Siente debilidad en los brazos, las piernas o ambos?
Do you feel weak in the arms, legs, or both?

 Brazos
Arms

 Piernas
Legs

 En ambos
Both

¿Cuándo comenzó la debilidad?
When did the weakness start?

MINUTOS	10	20	30	40	50	60				
MINUTES										

HORAS	2	4	6	8	10	12	14	16	18	20	22
HOURS											

DÍAS	1	2	3	4	5	6	7	8	9	10	>
DAYS											

SEMANAS	1	2	3	4	5	6	7	8	9	10	>
WEEKS											

MESES	1	2	3	4	5	6	7	8	9	10	>
MONTHS											

AÑOS	1	2	3	4	5	6	7	8	9	10	>
YEARS											

¿La debilidad inició de repente?
Did the weakness start suddenly?

¿La debilidad es constante o intermitente?
Is the weakness constant or does it come and go?

 Constante
Constant

 Intermitente
Comes and goes

NEUROLOGY

80

Muéstreme sus medicamentos si los tiene aquí.
Show me your medications, if you have them with you.

¿Tiene problemas de la vista?
Do you have vision problems?

¿Ha tenido recientemente pérdida de la visión, visión borrosa o visión doble?
Have you had a recent loss of vision, blurred vision, or double vision?

 Pérdida de la visión
Loss of Vision

 Visión doble
Double Vision

 Visión borrosa
Blurred Vision

¿Cuándo comenzaron los problemas de la visión?
When did the vision trouble start?

MINUTOS Minutes	10	20	30	40	50	60					
HORAS Hours	2	4	6	8	10	12	14	16	18	20	22
DÍAS Days	1	2	3	4	5	6	7	8	9	10	>
SEMANAS Weeks	1	2	3	4	5	6	7	8	9	10	>
MESES Months	1	2	3	4	5	6	7	8	9	10	>
AÑOS Years	1	2	3	4	5	6	7	8	9	10	>

¿Los problemas de visión comenzaron súbita o gradualmente?
Did the vision trouble start suddenly or gradually?

 De repente
Suddenly

 Gradualmente
Gradually

¿El problema de visión es constante o intermitente?
Is the vision trouble constant or does it come and go?

 Constante
Constant

 Intermitente
Comes and goes

¿El problema de visión es con un ojo o con ambos ojos?
Does the vision trouble involve one eye or both eyes?

 Izquierdo
Left

 Derecho
Right

 En ambos
Both

¿Tiene problemas viendo objetos de cerca, de lejos o ambos?
Do you have trouble seeing objects close, far away, or both?

 De cerca
Close

 De lejos
Far away

 Ambos
Both

¿Normalmente utiliza gafas, contactos o ambos?
Do you normally wear glasses, contact lenses, or both?

 Gafas
Glasses

 Contactos
Contact lenses

 Ambos
Both

NEUROLOGY

82
NEUROLOGIC PROCEDURAL

Por favor, sonría y muéstreme los dientes.
Please smile and show me your teeth.

Por favor, saque la lengua.
Please stick out your tongue.

Por favor, dé su nombre completo y diga donde nació, hablando tan fuerte y claramente como le sea posible.
Please say your full name and where you were born as loudly and as clearly as possible.

Por favor, ponga sus brazos rectos y manténgalos así cuando cierre los ojos.
Please hold your arms out straight and keep them straight when you close your eyes.

Por favor, apriéteme los dedos tan duro como le sea posible.
Please grip my fingers as tight as you can.

Por favor, presione contra mi mano con su pie.
Please push against my hand with your foot.

Por favor, hale su pie contra mi mano.
Please pull your foot up against my hand.

Por favor, encoja los hombros.
Please shrug your shoulders.

Con su dedo índice izquierdo toque mi dedo, luego tóquese la nariz.
With your left index finger touch my finger, then touch your nose.

Con su dedo índice derecho toque mi dedo, luego tóquese la nariz.
With your right index finger touch my finger, then touch your nose.

Doble la rodilla izquierda y coloque el talón del pie izquierdo contra la canilla de la pierna derecha.
Bend your left knee and place your left heel on your right shin.

Doble la rodilla derecha y coloque el talón del pie derecho contra la canilla de la pierna izquierda.
Bend your right knee and place your right heel on your left shin.

Con los ojos cerrados, dígame qué dedo de pie le estoy tocando. ¿Y ahora?
With your eyes closed, tell me what toe I am touching. How about now?
(Testing tactile stimuli to most distal extremities.)

¿Puede levantar la pierna izquierda y mantenerla así diez segundos?
Can you lift and hold your left leg up for me? (hold 10 seconds)

¿Puede levantar la pierna derecha y mantenerla así diez segundos?
Can you lift and hold your right leg up for me? (hold 10 seconds)

Por favor, camine en línea recta brevemente y devuélvase hacia mí.
Please walk in a straight line briefly and then walk back toward me.

Por favor, siga mi dedo/luz con los ojos.
Please follow my finger/light with your eyes.

Por favor, mire mi nariz y señale donde ve mis dedos moverse.
Please look at my nose and point to where you see my fingers wriggling.

NEUROLOGY

84
PAST NEUROLOGIC HISTORY

¿Ha sufrido una apoplejía (derrame) en el pasado?
Have you ever had a stroke in the past?

¿Cuánto hace que tuvo el derrame?
How long ago did you have the stroke?

DÍAS DAYS	1	2	3	4	5	6	7	8	9	10	>
SEMANAS WEEKS	1	2	3	4	5	6	7	8	9	10	>
MESES MONTHS	1	2	3	4	5	6	7	8	9	10	>
AÑOS YEARS	1	2	3	4	5	6	7	8	9	10	>

¿Usted visita a un neurólogo regularmente?
Do you regularly see a neurologist?

¿Está tomando algún tipo de medicamento para
prevenir derrames?
Are you on any medication to prevent stroke?

¿Ha tomado sus medicamentos hoy?
Did you take your medication today?

¿Se le han acabado sus medicamentos?
Have you run out of your medication?

¿Usted toma?:
Do you take:

Aspirina	✓	✕	Aspirin
Clopidogrel o Plavix	✓	✕	Clopidogrel or Plavix
Aggrenox	✓	✕	Aggrenox
Coumadin	✓	✕	Coumadin
Pradaxa	✓	✕	Pradaxa
Rivaroxaban o Xarelto	✓	✕	Rivaroxaban or Xarelto

- -

¿Cuándo fue la última vez que tomó sus medicamentos?
When did you last take your medication?

| **HORAS** | 2 | 4 | 6 | 8 | 10 | 12 | 14 | 16 | 18 | 20 | 22 |
| HOURS | | | | | | | | | | | |

| **DÍAS** | 1 | 2 | 3 | 4 | 5 | 6 | 7 | 8 | 9 | 10 | > |
| DAYS | | | | | | | | | | | |

¿Tiene una receta para medicamentos que todavía no ha obtenido?

Do you have a prescription for medication that you have not filled yet?

NEUROLOGY

¿En los últimos tres meses ha sufrido derrame/AIT?
In the past three months have you had a stroke/TIA?

¿Cuántos derrames/AIT ha sufrido?
How many strokes/TIAs have you had?

?   1   2   3   4   5   >

¿Cuándo comenzó el derrame tuvo ataque convulsivo?
Did you have a seizure when the stroke began?

¿Han mejorado los síntomas del derrame?
Are your stroke symptoms getting better?

¿Han desaparecido los síntomas del derrame?
Have your stroke symptoms gone away?

¿En los últimos tres meses ha sufrido un
traumatismo craneal?
In the past three months have you had a head trauma?

¿En los últimos tres meses ha sufrido un infarto?
In the past three months have you had a heart attack?

¿Ha sufrido recientemente de hemorragia
gastrointestinal o del tracto urinario?
Have you had a recent gastrointestinal or urinary tract hemorrhage?

¿Ha tenido una cirugía o un traumatismo en los
últimos 14 días?
Have you had surgery or a recent trauma within the past 14 days?

¿Alguna vez ha tenido sangrado o una ruptura arterial en el cerebro?
Have you ever had bleeding or a ruptured artery in the brain?

¿Tiene diabetes?
Do you have diabetes?

¿Fuma cigarrillos o usa tabaco de mascar?
Do you smoke cigarettes/cigars or use chewing tobacco?

¿Usted tiene la presión sanguínea alta?
Do you have high blood pressure?

¿Sufre de palpitaciones cardíacas irregulares?
Do you have an irregular heartbeat?

¿Tiene historial de fibrilación auricular?
Do you have a history of atrial fibrillation?

¿Tiene historial de embolia pulmonar?
Do you have a history of pulmonary embolisms?

¿Tiene historial de coágulos en la sangre?
Do you have a history of blood clots?

¿Tiene historial de meningitis?
Do you have a history of meningitis?

¿Tiene historial de convulciones?
Do you have a history of seizures?

¿Tiene historial de epilepsia?
Do you have a history of epilepsy?

OBSTETRICS

88

Hola, soy un(a) profesional de la salud. No hablo español.

Hello, I am a healthcare professional. I do not speak Spanish.

Respóndame solo sí o no ✖.

Only respond to me "yes" or "no."

ACUTE OBSTETRIC HISTORY

¿Está embarazada?
Are you pregnant?

¿Utilizó recientemente una prueba de embarazo en casa?
Did you recently use a home pregnancy test?

¿Algún médico ha confirmado recientemente que está embarazada?
Has a physician recently confirmed that you are pregnant?

¿Ya rompió fuente?
Has your water broken?

¿Tiene contracciones?
Are you having contractions?

¿El bebé ya viene ahora?
Is the baby coming now?

¿Siente dolor abdominal?
Do you have abdominal pain?

¿Siente dolor vaginal?
Do you have vaginal pain?

¿Tiene sangrado vaginal?
Do you have vaginal bleeding?

¿Tiene secreción vaginal anormal?
Do you have abnormal vaginal discharge?

¿Está usted en embarazo de alto riesgo?
Are you a high risk pregnancy?

¿Ha tenido alguna lesión física recientemente?
Have you had a recent physical injury?

OBSTETRIC PROCEDURAL

Por favor, cámbiese de ropa y póngase esta bata.
Please change out of your clothes and into this gown.

Por favor, acuéstese en la mesa y ponga los pies en los estribos.
Please lie down on the table and put your feet into the stirrups.

Por favor, baje un poco.
Please move down a bit.

Voy a colocarle suero. Va a sentir una punzada brevemente pero esto es importante hacerlo para poder administrarle medicamentos.
I am going to start an IV. This may sting briefly, but is important so we can give you medication.

Le voy a dar algo de oxígeno mediante el uso de una máscara que va en la cara o dentro la nariz. Puede ser incómodo. Por favor, relájese.
I am going to give you some oxygen either by a mask that goes over you face or up your nose. It may be uncomfortable. Please relax.

OBSTETRICS

PAST OBSTETRIC HISTORY

- -

Indique cuántas semanas han pasado desde la última menstruación.
Indicate how many weeks have passed since your last menstrual period.

| SEMANAS | 1 | 2 | 3 | 4 | 5 | 6 | 7 | 8 | 9 | 10 | > |
| WEEKS |

| MESES | 1 | 2 | 3 | 4 | 5 | 6 | 7 | 8 | 9 | 10 | > |
| MONTHS |

Indique cuántos meses tiene de embarazo.
Indicate how many months you have been pregnant.

| MESES | 1 | 2 | 3 | 4 | 5 | 6 | 7 | 8 | 9 | 10 | > |
| MONTHS |

Indique la fecha de su última menstruación.
Please indicate the date of your last menstrual period.

Enero January	Mayo May	Setiembre September	1	2	3	4	5	6	7
Febrero February	Junio June	Octubre October	8	9	10	11	12	13	14
			15	16	17	18	19	20	21
Marzo March	Julio July	Noviembre November	22	23	24	25	26	27	28
Abril April	Agosto August	Diciembre December	29	30	31				

Indique el número de veces que ha estado embarazada.
Indicate how many times you have been pregnant.

1 2 3 4 5 6 7 8 9 10 >

Indique el número de hijos que tiene.
Indicate how many children you have.

1 2 3 4 5 6 7 8 9 10 >

Indique el número de abortos provocados o abortos espontáneos que haya tenido.
Indicate how many abortions or miscarriages you have had.

1 2 3 4 5 6 7 8 9 10 >

¿Alguna vez ha tenido un embarazo ectópico anterior?
Have you ever had a previous ectopic pregnancy?

¿Ha tenido complicaciones con un embarazo anterior?
Have you had complications with a past pregnancy?

¿Ha tenido un niño con problemas mentales o físicos?
Have you had a child with mental and/or physical handicaps?

¿Ha tenido un niño que nació prematuramente?
Have you had a child that was delivered prematurely?

¿Ha tenido un niño que necesitó cirugía después de haber nacido?
Have you had a child that required surgery after being born?

Hola, soy un(a) profesional de la salud. No hablo español.

Hello, I am a healthcare professional. I do not speak Spanish.

Respóndame solo sí o no .

Only respond to me "yes" or "no."

ACUTE ONCOLOGICAL HISTORY

¿Padece actualmente de cáncer?

Do you currently have cancer?

Por favor señale (en este dibujo de una persona) donde tiene cáncer.

Please point (on this picture of a person) to where you have cancer.

¿Hace metástasis?

Do you have metastases?

¿Cuándo le diagnosticaron el cáncer?
When was your cancer diagnosed?

Enero January	Mayo May	Setiembre September	1	2	3	4	5	6	7
Febrero February	Junio June	Octubre October	8	9	10	11	12	13	14
Marzo March	Julio July	Noviembre November	15 16 17 18 19 20 21 22 23 24 25 26 27 28
Abril April	Agosto August	Diciembre December	29 30 31

¿Está recibiendo quimioterapia/radioterapia para el cáncer?

Are you currently receiving chemotherapy/radiation for the cancer?

ACUTE ONCOLOGICAL HISTORY

Voy a acceder a su Porta-cath.
I am going to acces your Porta-cath

Necesito que se ponga esta máscara en la cara.
I need you to put this mask on your face.

Voy a colocarle suero. Va a sentir una punzada brevemente pero esto es importante hacerlo para poder administrarle medicamentos.
I am going to start an IV. This may sting briefly, but is important so we can give you medication.

ONCOLOGY

94

PAST ONCOLOGICAL HISTORY

¿Había tenido cáncer anteriormente?
Have you previously had cancer?

Por favor, señale en este dibujo donde tuvo cáncer.
Please point on this picture where you had cancer.

¿Hizo metástasis?
Did you have metastases?

¿Cuándo le diagnosticaron el cáncer?
When was your cancer diagnosed?

Enero January	Mayo May	Setiembre September	1	2	3	4	5	6	7
Febrero February	Junio June	Octubre October	8	9	10	11	12	13	14
			15	16	17	18	19	20	21
Marzo March	Julio July	Noviembre November	22	23	24	25	26	27	28
Abril April	Agosto August	Diciembre December	29	30	31				

¿Su cáncer está en remisión?
Is the cancer in remission?

¿Tiene un familiar que tenga cáncer?
Do you have a family member who has cancer?

¿Algún familiar suyo ha fallecido a causa de cáncer?
Do you have a family member who has died due to cancer?

¿Fuma cigarrillos o utiliza productos de tabaco?
Do you smoke cigarettes or use tobacco products?

 Sí
Yes

 No
No

 Dejé de fumar
I quit

¿Ha tenido un resultado positivo en la prueba de la tuberculosis?
Have you had a positive test for tuberculosis?

Hola, soy un(a) profesional de la salud. No hablo español.

Hello, I am a healthcare professional. I do not speak Spanish.

Respóndame solo sí o no .

Only respond to me "yes" or "no."

ACUTE OPHTHALMOLOGICAL HISTORY

¿Tiene problemas de la vista?

Are you having vision problems?

¿En qué ojo?

Which eye?

 Izquierdo
Left

 Derecho
Right

 En ambos
Both

¿Le duelen los ojos?

Do your eyes hurt?

¿Qué ojo le duele?

Which eye hurts?

 Izquierdo
Left

 Derecho
Right

 Ambos
Both

¿Tiene doble visión?
Do you have double vision?

¿La doble visión desaparece cuando cierra un ojo?
Does the double vision go away when you close one eye?

¿La luz le molesta los ojos?
Does light bother your eyes?

¿Comenzó el dolor cuando pasó a la luz?
Did the pain start when you went into light?

¿Comenzó el dolor cuando pasó a la oscuridad?
Did the pain start when you went into the dark?

¿Tiene algún traumatismo reciente en los ojos?
Did you have any recent trauma to your eyes?

 Sí, en el izquierdo
Yes, left

 Sí, en ambos
Yes, both

 Sí, en el derecho
Yes, right

 No
No

¿Tiene el ojo rojo?
Is the eye red?

¿Siente dolor en un lado de la cabeza?
Is there any pain on the side of your head?

 Sí, en el izquierdo
Yes, left

 Sí, en ambos
Yes, both

 Sí, en el derecho
Yes, right

 No
No

OPHTHALMOLOGY

98

¿Tiene destellos de luz en la vista?
Do you have any flashes of light in your vision?

¿Ve alguna cosa flotando en la vista?
Do you have anything floating in your vision?

¿Puede ver en todas las áreas de su campo de visión?
Can you see in all sections of your field of vision?

¿Siente como si tuviera una cortina en su campo de visión?
Do you feel like there is a curtain across your field of vision?

¿Ha tenido la presión alta recientemente?
Has your blood pressure recently been high?

¿Usa colirio para los ojos?
Do you use any eyedrops?

¿La vista le causa dolor de cabeza?
Do you have a headache with your vision?

¿Siente náuseas/vómitos con los cambios en la visión?
Do you have any nausea/vomiting with vision changes?

¿Ve las cosas borrosas?
Are things blurry?

¿Las cosas que están lejos las ve borrosas?
Are things that are far away blurry?

¿Las cosas que están cerca las ve borrosas?
Are things that are close blurry?

OPHTHALMOLOGIC PROCEDURAL

Voy a señalar un renglón con letras. Por favor, dígame que letras son.
I am going to point to a line of letters. Please repeat those letters out loud.

Por favor, siga mi dedo/luz con los ojos.
Please follow my fingers/light with your eyes.

Voy a ponerle gotas en los ojos. Esto puede ser un poco incómodo.
I'm going to place eyedrops in your eye. This may be briefly uncomfortable.

PAST OPHTHALMOLOGICAL HISTORY

¿Usa gafas?
Do you wear glasses?
   No, pero usaba
No, but I used to

¿Usa contactos?
Do you wear contacts?

 Sí, en el izquierdo
Yes, left

 Sí, en ambos
Yes, both

 Sí, en el derecho
Yes, right

 No
No

¿Tiene glaucoma?
Do you have glaucoma?

¿Tiene historial de migrañas?
Do you have a history of migraines?

¿Ha sufrido recientemente un traumatismo en la cabeza?
Have you had any recent head trauma?

PSYCHIATRY/PSYCHOLOGY

100

Hola, soy un(a) profesional de la salud. No hablo español.

Hello, I am a healthcare professional. I do not speak Spanish.

Respóndame solo sí o no .

Only respond to me "yes" or "no."

ACUTE PSYCHIATRIC/PSYCHOLOGICAL HISTORY

¿Se siente triste o deprimido?

Do you feel sad or depressed?

¿Tiene la sensación de querer hacerse daño
físicamente a si mismo u a otras personas?

Do you have feelings of wanting to physically hurt yourself or others?

¿Tiene planeado hacerse daño físicamente a
si mismo u a otras personas?

Do you have a plan to physically hurt yourself or others?

¿Padece actualmente de ansiedad?

Do you currently have anxiety?

¿Se preocupa constantemente?

Do you worry constantly?

¿Teme que alguien le haga daño?

Are you afraid of someone harming you?

¿Tiene sentimientos abrumadores de culpa?

Do you feel overwhelming guilt?

PSYCHIATRIC/PSYCHOLOGICAL PROCEDURAL

Por favor, cámbiese de ropa y póngase esta bata.
Please change out of your clothes and into this gown.

Por favor, tómese este medicamento con agua.
Please take this oral medication and swallow with water.

Vamos a administrarle un medicamento por vía intravenosa o intramuscular.
We are going to give you some medication through your IV or into your muscles.

PAST PSYCHIATRIC/PSYCHOLOGICAL HISTORY

¿Bebe más de cinco bebidas alcohólicas al día?
Do you drink more than five alcoholic drinks a day?

 Sí
Yes

 No
No

 Dejé el trago
I quit

Por favor, indique el tipo de bebida alcohólica que normalmente consume.
Please indicate type of alcohol you normally drink.

 Cerveza
Beer

Whiskey
Whiskey

Vodka
Vodka

 Bourbon
Bourbon

Vino
Wine

 Otra
Other

 Ginebra
Gin

¿Fuma cigarrillos o utiliza productos de tabaco?

Do you smoke cigarettes or use tobacco products?

 Sí
Yes

 No
No

 Dejé de fumar
I quit

¿Utiliza alguna droga ilícita o medicamentos que
no fueron prescritos para usted?

Do you use any illicit drugs/medications that were not prescribed to you?

 Sí
Yes

 No
No

 Dejé las drogas
I quit

Por favor, indique qué tipo de drogas utiliza.

Please indicate what type of drugs you use.

 Cocaína
Cocaine

 Éxtasis
Ecstasy

 Heroína
Heroin

 LSD/ "ácido"
LSD/"acid"

 Marihuana
Marijuana

Metanfetaminas
Methamphetamines

Otra
Other

Por favor, indique de qué forma usa estas drogas.
Please indicate in which form you use these drugs.

Inyectada por vía intravenosa
Inject intravenously

Introducida por vía rectal
Insert rectally

Fumada
Smoke

Aspirada por la nariz
Snort

Por vía oral en forma de píldora
Swallow in pill form

Otra
Other

¿Ha sufrido antes de maltrato físico?
Have you been physically abused before?

¿Ha sufrido antes de abuso sexual?
Have you been sexually abused before?

¿Ha sufrido antes de abuso emocional?
Have you been emotionally abused before?

PSYCHIATRY/PSYCHOLOGY

104

¿Usted toma medicamentos para la ansiedad?
Do you take medication for anxiety?

Sí, regularmente
Yes, regularly.

 No
No

Sí, pero no soy constante.
Yes, but I am not consistent.

Un médico me ha recetado medicamentos para la ansiedad pero no los tomo.
I have been prescribed medication for anxiety by a physician but do not take it.

¿Usted toma medicamentos para el trastorno bipolar?
Do you take medication for Bi-Polar Disorder?

Sí, regularmente
Yes, regularly.

 No
No

Sí, pero no soy constante.
Yes, but I am not consistent.

Un médico me ha recetado medicamentos para el trastorno bipolar pero no los tomo.
I have been prescribed medication for Bi-Polar Disorder by a physician but do not take it.

¿Usted toma medicamentos para la depresión?
Do you take medication for depression?

✓ **Sí, regularmente**
Yes, regularly.

✗ No
No

✓ **Sí, pero no soy constante.**
Yes, but I am not consistent.

✓ **Un médico me ha recetado medicamentos para la depresión pero no los tomo.**
I have been prescribed medication for depression by a physician but do not take it.

¿Usted toma medicamentos para la esquizofrenia?
Do you take medication for schizophrenia?

✓ **Sí, regularmente**
Yes, regularly.

 No
No

✓ **Sí, pero no soy constante.**
Yes, but I am not consistent.

✓ **Un médico me ha recetado medicamentos para la esquizofrenia pero no los tomo.**
I have been prescribed medication for schizophrenia by a physician but do not take it.

PULMONOLOGY

106

ACUTE PULMONOLOGICAL HISTORY

¿Tiene dificultad para respirar?
Do you have shortness of breath?

¿Cuándo comenzó la dificultad para respirar?
When did your shortness of breath begin?

DÍAS   1   2   3   4   5   6   7   8   9   10   >
DAYS

¿Siente dolor en el pecho?
Do you have chest pain?

Por favor, señale sobre su propio pecho exactamente donde siente dolor.
Please point on your own chest to where you have chest pain.

¿Le duele respirar?
Does it hurt to breathe?

¿Utiliza un inhalador de dosis medida (IDM) en casa?
Do you use a metered dose inhaler (MDI) at home?

 Sí
Yes

 Sí, pero se me acabó medicamento.
Yes, but I ran out of medication.

 No
No

¿Cuándo fue la última vez que usó el inhalador de dosis medida (IDM)?
When was the last time you used your metered dose inhaler (MDI)?

DÍAS 1 2 3 4 5 6 7 8 9 10 >
DAYS

¿Cuántas veces ha usado el inhalador de dosis medida (IDM) hoy?
How many times have you used your metered dose inhaler (MDI) today?

1 2 3 4 5 6 7 8 9 10 >

¿El inhalador de dosis medida le sirve cuando siente que le falta el aire?
Did the metered dose inhaler help your shortness of breath?

✓ **Sí**
Yes

✗ **No**
No

✓ **Un poco**
A little

¿Usted utiliza un espaciador o cámara con el inhalador de dosis medida (IDM)?
Do you use a spacer/chamber with your metered dose inhaler (MDI)?

 Sí
Yes

✗ **No**
No

 Sí, a veces
Yes, sometimes

¿Tiene congestión nasal?
Do you have nasal congestion?

PULMONOLOGY

108

¿Tiene tos?
Do you have a cough?

¿Tiene esputo al toser? *flema*
Are you coughing up any sputum?

¿De qué color es el esputo?
What color is your sputum?

 Marrón
Brown

 Rojo
Red

 Verde
Green

 Amarillo
Yellow

 Negro
Black

¿Hay sangre presente en el esputo?
Is there any blood in your sputum?

¿Alguna vez ha sido encarcelado o
ha estado en una prisión?
Have you ever been incarcerated/in prison?

¿Ha estado expuesto a la tuberculosis?
Have you been exposed to tuberculosis?

¿La tos cambia al cambiar el clima?
Does your cough change with the weather?

PULMONOLOGIC PROCEDURAL

. . . .

Por favor, quítese la ropa y póngase esta bata.
Please change out of your clothes and into this gown.

Necesito escuchar sus pulmones. Por favor, respire normalmente.
I need to listen to your lungs. Please breathe normally.

Necesito escuchar sus pulmones. Por favor, respire profundo y despacio.
I need to listen to your lungs. Please breathe deeply and slowly.

Le voy a administrar oxígeno por la nariz. Esto puede ser un poco incómodo.
I am going to give you oxygen through your nose.
This may be mildly uncomfortable.

Le voy a dar oxígeno a través de esta máscara que se coloca sobre la boca y la nariz. Esto puede ser un poco incómodo.
I am going to give you oxygen through this mask that will will go over your mouth and nose. This may be mildly uncomfortable.

Le voy a colocar un ventilador de presión positiva en modo CPAP o uno de ventilación no invasiva en modo BiPAP. Se siente como si usted hubiera sacado la cabeza por la ventana de un carro en movimiento y será brevemente incómodo.
I am going to put you on a CPAP or BiPAP. It will feel like your head is outside the window of a moving car and will be uncomfortable for a little bit.

. . . .

PULMONOLOGY

110

Le voy a administrar medicamento mediante un inhalador que calibra la dosis. Esto no le va a doler.

I am going to give you medication through a metered dose inhaler. This will not hurt.

 Por favor, exhale totalmente.
Please exhale completely.

 Por favor, inhale profundamente.
Please inhale deeply.

Le voy a administrar medicamento mediante un nebulizador. Esto no le va a doler. Por favor, inhale lenta y profundamente.

I am going to give you medication through a nebulizer. This will not hurt. Please inhale slowly and deeply.

Past Pulmonological History

¿Tiene historial de asma?
Do you have a history of asthma?

 Sí
Yes

 No
No

 Sí, pero solo cuando niño.
Yes, but only as a child.

¿Alguna vez lo han entubado (un tubo en la garganta para ayudarle a respirar) debido a su asma?
Have you ever been intubated (a tube down your throat to help you breathe) because of your asthma?

¿Cuántas veces ha sido entubado?
How many times have you been intubated?

1 2 3 4 5 6 7 8 9 10 >

¿Usted utiliza un espaciador o cámara con el inhalador de dosis medida (IDM)?
Do you use a spacer/chamber with your metered dose inhaler (MDI)?

 Sí
Yes

 No
No

 No, pero antes tenía.
No, but I used to.

¿Usted toma corticosteroides para el asma?
Do you take corticosteroids for your asthma?

 Sí
Yes

 No
No

 No, pero usaba antes.
No, but I used to.

¿Ha estado en la unidad de cuidados intensivos (UCI) por causa del asma?

Have you been in the intensive care unit (ICU) for your asthma?

¿Cuántas veces ha sido internado en un hospital debido al asma?
How many times have you been admitted to a hospital due to your asthma?

1 2 3 4 5 6 7 8 9 10 >

PULMONOLOGY

112

¿Tiene historial de?:

Do you have a history of:

Fibrilación auricular			Atrial fibrillation
Bronquitis			Bronchitis
Enfermedad pulmonar obstructiva crónica			Chronic obstructive pulmonary disease
Insuficiencia cardíaca congestiva			Congestive heart failure
Enfisema			Emphysema
Neumonía			Pneumonia
Edema pulmonar			Pulmonary edema
Embolia pulmonar			Pulmonary embolisms
Tuberculosis			Tuberculosis

¿Tiene implantado un marcapasos o desfibrilador?

Do you have an implanted pacemaker/defibrillator?

Hola, soy un(a) profesional de la salud. No hablo español.

Hello, I am a healthcare professional. I do not speak Spanish.

Respóndame solo sí o no .

Only respond to me "yes" or "no."

ACUTE RENAL HISTORY

¿Tiene problemas renales (de riñones)?

Do you have renal (kidney) problems?

¿Se somete a tratamientos de diálisis?

Do you take dialysis treatments?

¿Cuál es su programa de diálisis normal?

What is your normal dialysis schedule?

 lunes, miércoles y viernes

Monday, Wednesday, Friday

 martes, jueves y sábado

Tuesday, Thursday, Saturday

¿Perdió su cita más reciente?

Have you missed your most recent appointment?

¿Cuándo fue la última vez que se sometió a tratamiento de diálisis?
When was the last time you had your dialysis treatment?

| MINUTOS | 10 | 20 | 30 | 40 | 50 | 60 | | | | |
| MINUTES | | | | | | | | | | |

| HORAS | 2 | 4 | 6 | 8 | 10 | 12 | 14 | 16 | 18 | 20 | 22 |
| HOURS | | | | | | | | | | | |

| DÍAS | 1 | 2 | 3 | 4 | 5 | 6 | 7 | 8 | 9 | 10 | > |
| DAYS | | | | | | | | | | | |

RENAL PROCEDURAL

Por favor, use este colador para la orina.
Please use this urine strainer.

Voy a acceder a la válvula de derivación.
I am going to access your shunt.

Voy a empezar su diálisis.
I am going to start your dialysis.

Voy a parar su diálisis.
I am going to stop your dialysis.

Su diálisis está completo. Voy a descargar el acceso
a la válvula de derivación.
Your dialysis treatment is complete. I am going to
discharge your port access.

PAST RENAL HISTORY

¿Tiene historial de insuficiencia renal?
Do you have a history of renal failure (kidney failure)?

¿Le han tenido que extirpar un riñón?
Have you had a kidney removed?

¿Qué riñón?
Which kidney?
 Izquierdo
Left
 Derecho
Right

¿Le han tenido que hacer trasplante de riñón?
Have you had a kidney transplant?

¿Qué riñón?
Which kidney?

 Izquierdo
Left

 Derecho
Right

 Ambos
Both

¿Usted toma medicación inmunosupresora?
Do you take immunosuppressant medication?

¿Tiene historial de cálculos renales?
Do you have a history of kidney stones?

¿Lo han vacunado a usted contra la
Hepatitis B (HepB)?

Have you had your Hepatitis B (HepB) vaccine?

¿Lo han vacunado a usted contra la
Hepatitis A (HepA)?

Have you had your Hepatitis A (HepA) vaccine?

¿Lo han vacunado a usted contra la difteria,
el tétano y contra la tos ferina (DTPA)?

Have you had your Diphtheria and tetanus toxoids and
acellular pertussis vaccine (DTaP)?

¿Lo han vacunado contra el rotavirus (RV)?

Have you had your Rotavirus vaccine (RV)?

¿Lo han vacunado contra el poliovirus (IPV)?

Have you had your inactivate poliovirus
vaccine (IPV)?

¿Le han aplicado la vacuna conjugada contra
la Haemophilus influenzae tipo b (Hib/HbCV)?

Have you had your Haemophilus Influenzae Type B
conjugate vaccine (Hib/HbCV) Immunization?

¿Lo han vacunado contra
el resfriado (estacional)?

Have you had your influenza vaccine (seasonal)?

¿Le han aplicado la vacuna antimeningocócica conjugada, tetravalente (MCV4)?
Have you had your Meningococcal conjugate vaccine, quadrivalent (MCV4) vaccine?

¿Le han aplicado la vacuna triple vírica (sarampión, paperas y rubéola)?
Have you had your MMR (measles, mumps, and rubella) vaccine?

¿Lo han vacunado contra el neumococo (VCN)?
Have you had your Pneumococcal vaccine (PCV)?

¿Lo han vacunado contra el virus del papiloma humano (VPH)?
Have you had your human papillomavirus vaccine (HPV)?

¿Le han hecho la prueba de tuberculina (PPD)?
Have you had your tuberculin skin test (PPD)?

¿Arrojó resultado positivo o negativo?
Was it negative or positive?

¿Se ha vacunado contra el tétano en los últimos 10 años?
Have you had a tetanus vaccine within the last 10 years?

¿Se ha vacunado contra el resfriado en el último año?
Have you had an influenza vaccine within the last year?

¿La vacuna contra la neumonía neumocócica está al día?

Is your pneumococcal pneumonia vaccine up to date?

Por favor, anote el nombre de su médico de cabecera.

Please write the name of your primary care physician or provider.

 No tengo médico de cabecera o proveedor médico.

I don't have a primary care physician or provider.

Por favor, anote la dirección de su médico de cabecera.

Please write the address of your primary care physician or provider.

_____

Calle (Street)   Apartamento (Apt. #)

_____

Ciudad (City)   Estado (State)   Código Postal (ZIP)

Por favor, anote el número de teléfono de su médico de cabecera.

Please write the phone number of your primary care physician or provider.

(_____) _____ – _____

TB SCREENING

¿Ha tenido usted tos prolongada por 3 semanas o más?
Have you had a prolonged cough for 3 weeks or more?

¿Ha tenido pérdida de peso inexplicable?
Have you had unexplained weight loss?

¿Ha tenido usted fiebre y escalofríos recientemente?
Have you had a recent fever/chills?

¿Ha visto usted sangre en el esputo?
Have you had any blood in your sputum?

¿Ha sido alguna vez indigente o ha estado sin hogar?
Have you ever been homeless?

¿Tiene o ha tenido historial de tuberculosis activa en algún momento?
Do you have a history of active tuberculosis now or at anytime?

¿Ha arrojado resultados positivos en la prueba contra la tuberculosis en los últimos 2 años?
Have you had a positive tuberculosis test within the past 2 years?

¿Tiene bomba de insulina?
Do you have an insulin pump?

¿Tiene redactado un documento de instrucciones anticipadas?
Do you have an advance directive?

SCREENINGS-ADULT

120

¿Desea asistencia para redactar instrucciones anticipadas?
Do you want assistance with an advance directive?

¿Está usted seguro en el entorno de su casa?
Are you safe in your home environment?

¿Desea que nos pongamos en contacto con
cuidado pastoral?
Do you want us to contact Pastoral Care?

¿Desea que nos pongamos en contacto con
Servicios Sociales?
Do you want us to contact Social Services?

¿Desea que nos pongamos en contacto
con un intérprete?
Do you want us to contact an interpreter?

¿Desea que nosotros ó el intérprete contacte a un pariente?
Do you want us/the interpreter to contact a family member?

Este familiar es:
This family member is a:

 Esposo(a)
Spouse

 Hijo(a)
Child

 Padre o Madre
Parent

 Otro pariente
Other relative

Anote el número de teléfono del pariente:
Please write down their phone number: (_____) _____ - _____

FOR CAREGIVER/FAMILY/WITNESS

¿El paciente tiene un historial de confusión o la demencia?
Does the patient have a history of confusion or dementia?

¿El paciente tiene historial de deterioro en la capacidad cognitiva?
Does the patient have a history of impaired cognitive ability?

¿El paciente es un peligro para sí mismo o los demás?
Is the patient a danger to self or others?

¿El paciente tiene historial de fuga?
Does the patient have a history of wandering off?

¿El paciente expresa su intención de irse?
Does the patient verbalize an attempt to leave?

¿El paciente tiene alguna de las siguientes necesidades especiales?
Does the patient have any of the following special needs?

 Cultural
Cultural

 Emocional
Emotional

 Aflicción
Grief

  Pérdida
Loss

 Personal
Personal

 Religiosa
Religious

 Social
Social

 Otro
Other

No lo sé.
I don't know.

¿El paciente tiene alguna de las siguientes barreras de aprendizaje?
Does the patient have any of the following learning barriers?

✓ **Cognitiva**
Cognitive

✓ **Aprendizaje**
Learning

✓ **Educación**
Education

✓ **Otro**
Other

✓ **Audición**
Hearing

✓ **No lo sé.**
I don't know.

¿Cuándo fue la última fecha en la que el paciente fue visto por última vez normal/bien?
When was the last date the patient seemed normal/well?

Enero / January	Mayo / May	Setiembre / September
Febrero / February	Junio / June	Octubre / October
Marzo / March	Julio / July	Noviembre / November
Abril / April	Agosto / August	Diciembre / December

1 2 3 4 5 6 7
8 9 10 11 12 13 14
15 16 17 18 19 20 21
22 23 24 25 26 27 28
29 30 31

¿Cuándo fue la última vez (hoy) en la que el paciente fue visto por última vez normal/bien?
When was the last time (today) the patient seemed normal/well?

AM 1 2 3 4 5 6 7 8 9 10 11 12

PM 1 2 3 4 5 6 7 8 9 10 11 12

Hola, soy un(a) profesional de la salud. No hablo español.
Hello, I am a healthcare professional. I do not speak Spanish.

¿Siente dolor?
Do you have pain?

Por favor, señale (en este dibujo de una persona) donde tiene dolor.
Please point (on this picture of a person) to where you have pain.

124

¿Cuándo comenzó el dolor?
When did your pain begin?

MINUTOS MINUTES	10	20	30	40	50	60					
HORAS HOURS	2	4	6	8	10	12	14	16	18	20	22
DÍAS DAYS	1	2	3	4	5	6	7	8	9	10	>
SEMANAS WEEKS	1	2	3	4	5	6	7	8	9	10	>
MESES MONTHS	1	2	3	4	5	6	7	8	9	10	>
AÑOS YEARS	1	2	3	4	5	6	7	8	9	10	>

¿Cómo describiría el inicio del dolor?
How would you describe the onset of your pain?

Lo despertó al estar dormido
Awakened from sleep

Gradual
Gradual

Continuo
Ongoing

Progresivo
Progressive

Repentino
Sudden

No lo sé.
I don't know.

¿Qué hace que empeore el dolor?
What makes the pain worse?

Al defecar
Bowel Movement

Al respirar
Breathing

Al comer
Eating

Al moverse
Movement

Al estar parado
Standing

Al tocarse o que lo toquen
Touch

Al orinar
Urination

Al caminar
Walking

¿Puede indicarme los movimientos que hacen que el dolor empeore?
Can you show me the movements that make your pain worse?

¿Qué hace que el dolor disminuya?
What makes the pain better?

Al moverse
Movement

Al posicionarse
Positioning

Medicamentos
Medications

El hielo/el frío
Ice/Cold

El calor
Heat

La actividad
Activity

¿Qué actividades hacen que el dolor mejor?
What activities make your pain better?

¿Cómo describiría el dolor?
How would you describe your pain?

✓ **Que duele**
Aching

✓ **Abrazador**
Burning

✓ **Con espasmos**
Cramping

✓ **Devastador**
Crushing

✓ **Que incomoda**
Discomfort

✓ **Sordo**
Dull

✓ **Que produce pesadez**
Heaviness

✓ **Que produce picazón**
Itching

✓ **En oleadas punzantes**
Jabbing

✓ **Persistente**
Nagging

✓ **Que acalambra**
Numbness

✓ **Penetrante**
Penetrating

✓ **Con palpitaciones**
Pounding

✓ **Que ocasiona presión**
Pressure

✓ **Que desgarra**
Ripping

✓ **Que irradia**
Radiating

✓ **Agudo**
Sharp

✓ **Fulgurante**
Shooting

✓ **Que resiente**
Sore

✓ **Que causa espasmos**
Spasms

✓ **Que aprieta**
Squeezing

✓ **Lacerante**
Stabbing

✓ **Que desgarra**
Tearing

✓ **Sensible**
Tender

✓ **Palpitante**
Throbbing

✓ **Que oprime**
Tightness

✓ **Que cansa**
Tiring

✓ **No puedo describirlo.**
I can't describe it.

¿El dolor irradia o se traslada a otra área de su cuerpo?
Does the pain radiate or move to another area of your body?

Si el dolor se irradia, por favor señale sobre su propio cuerpo donde se traslada.
If the pain radiates, please point on your own body where it goes.

. . . .

Por favor, indique (en la siguiente escala) la intensidad de su dolor.
Please point (on this scale) to rate your pain.

No hay dolor   Dolor moderado   Dolor intenso

0   1   2   3   4   5   6   7   8   9   10

. . . .

¿El dolor es constante o intermitente?
Is the pain constant or does it come and go?

 Constante
Constant

 Intermitente
Comes and goes

HEAD

- -

Voy a tocarle la cara. Esto puede ser un poco incómodo.
I am going to touch your face. This may be slightly uncomfortable.

Por favor, levante las cejas.
Please raise your eyebrows.

Por favor, abra los ojos.
Please open your eyes.

Por favor, cierre los ojos.
Please close your eyes.

Voy a ponerle una luz en los ojos.
I am going to shine a light in your eyes. This may be slightly uncomfortable.

Por favor, siga mi dedo/luz con los ojos.
Please follow my finger/light with your eyes.

Por favor, abra la boca.
Please open your mouth.

Por favor, cierre la boca.
Please close your mouth.

Por favor, déme una sonrisa amplia y muéstreme los dientes.
Please smile wide and show me your teeth.

Por favor, frunza el ceño.
Please frown.

Le voy a examinar los oídos. Esto puede ser un poco incómodo.
I am going to examine your ears. This may be slightly uncomfortable.

NECK

Le voy a tocar el cuello. Esto puede ser un poco incómodo.
I am going to touch your neck. This may be slightly uncomfortable.

Por favor, mire hacia el cielo raso.
Please look up at the ceiling.

Por favor, mire hacia abajo y tóquese el pecho con el mentón.
Please look down, bringing your chin to your chest.

Por favor, gire la cabeza a la izquierda por encima del hombro.
Please look over your shoulder to the left.

Por favor, gire la cabeza a la derecha por encima del hombro.
Please look over your shoulder to the right.

Por favor, tóquese el hombro izquierdo con la oreja.
Please bring your left ear to your left shoulder.

Por favor, tóquese el hombro derecho con la oreja.
Please bring your right ear to your right shoulder.

SHOULDERS

Le voy a tocar los hombros y/o la parte superior de la espalda.
Esto puede ser un poco incómodo.
I am going to touch your shoulders and/or upper back.
This may be slightly uncomfortable.

Por favor, levante los hombros hacia los oídos.
Please lift your shoulders toward your ears.

Por favor, levante los brazos hacia delante por encima de la cabeza.
Please lift your arms forward over your head.

Por favor, coloque los brazos hacia atrás.
Please reach your arms backwards.

Por favor, levante los brazos a los lados por encima de la cabeza.
Please lift your arms out to the sides over your head.

Por favor, dese usted mismo una palmadita en la espalda.
Please pat yourself on your back.

Por favor, trate de tocarse la espalda.
Please reach behind your back.

CHEST

Voy a tocarle el pecho. Esto puede ser un poco incómodo.
I am going to touch your chest. This may be slightly uncomfortable.

Tengo que escuchar los pulmones. Por favor, respire normalmente.
I need to listen to your lungs. Please breathe normally.

Tengo que escuchar los pulmones. Por favor, respire profunda y lentamente.
I need to listen to your lungs. Please breath deeply and slowly.

EVALUATION

132

ABDOMEN/GROIN

. . . .

Voy a tocarle el abdomen. Esto puede ser un poco incómodo.
I am going to touch your abdomen. This may be slightly uncomfortable.

Voy a escuchar el abdomen. Esto puede ser un poco incómodo.
I am going to listen to your abdomen. This will not hurt.

Por favor, inclínese hacia adelante.
Please lean forward.

Voy a tocarle el área de la ingle. Esto puede ser un poco incómodo.
I am going to touch your groin. This may be slightly uncomfortable.

SPINE

. . . .

Voy a tocarle la espalda y columna vertebral.
Esto puede ser un poco incómodo.
I am going to touch your back/spine. This may be slightly uncomfortable.

Por favor, muévase hacia atrás.
Please move backwards.

. . . .

Por favor, trate de llegar hasta el piso como si se fuera a tocar los dedos de los pies.
Please reach to the floor, as if to touch your toes.

Por favor, extiéndase hacia atrás.
Please extend backwards.

Por favor, inclínese a la izquierda y deslice la mano hacia abajo sobre la pierna izquierda.
Please bend to the left sliding your hand down the side of your left leg.

Por favor, inclínese a la derecha y deslice la mano hacia abajo sobre la pierna derecha.
Please bend to the right sliding your hand down the side of your right leg.

Por favor, tuerza la columna hacia la izquierda manteniendo la cadera hacia delante.
Please twist your spine to the left, keeping your hips forward.

Por favor, tuerza la columna hacia la derecha manteniendo la cadera hacia adelante.
Please twist your spine to the right, keeping your hips forward.

HIPS/LEGS

Voy a tocarle las caderas. Esto puede ser un poco incómodo.
I am going to touch your hips. This may be slightly uncomfortable.

Voy a tocarle las nalgas. Esto puede ser un poco incómodo.
I am going to touch your buttocks. This may be slightly uncomfortable.

Voy a tocarle las piernas. Esto puede ser un poco incómodo.
I am going to touch your legs. This may be slightly uncomfortable.

Por favor, levante la rodilla hacia el cielo raso. (Sentado)
Please lift your knee to the ceiling.

Por favor, levante la pierna de la estera. (Decúbito prono)
Por favor, mueva el pie hacia adentro. (Decúbito prono)
Please lift your leg off of the mat. Please bring your foot inward.

Por favor, mueva el pie hacia afuera. (Decúbito prono)
Please bring your foot outward.

Por favor, mueva la pierna hacia afuera, lejos de usted. (Decúbito supino)
Please move your leg outward, away from you.

Por favor, mueva la pierna hacia adentro,
hacia la otra pierna. (Decúbito supino)
Please move your leg inward, toward your other leg.

KNEES

Por favor, enderece la rodilla.
Please straighten your knee.

Por favor, doble la rodilla.
Please bend your knee back.

FEET/ANKLES

Voy a tocarle los pies. Esto puede ser un poco incómodo.
I am going to touch your feet. This may be slightly uncomfortable.

Por favor, separe los dedos de los pies.
Please spread your toes out.

Por favor, junte los dedos de los pies.
Please bring your toes together.

Por favor, apunte hacia arriba con los dedos de los pies.
Please point your toes up.

Por favor, apunte hacia abajo con los dedos de los pies.
Please point your toes down.

Por favor, mueva los dedos de los pies.
Please wiggle your toes.

Por favor, mueva el pie hacia arriba, trayéndolo hacia la cabeza.
Please move your foot up, bringing it toward your head.

Por favor, mueva el pie hacia abajo, como si fuera pisar el pedal del acelerador.
Please move your foot down, as if you are pushing on the gas pedal.

Por favor, mueva el pie hacia adentro.
Please bring your foot inward.

Por favor, mueva el pie hacia afuera.
Please bring your foot outward.

ARMS

Voy a tocarle los brazos. Esto puede ser un poco incómodo.
I am going to touch your arms. This may be slightly uncomfortable.

Por favor, doble/flexione el codo.
Please bend/flex your elbow.

Por favor, enderece el codo.
Please straighten your elbow.

Por favor, mantenga los brazos hacia adelante.
Please hold your arms forward.

Por favor, cierre los ojos y mantenga los brazos hacia delante.
Please close your eyes and keep your arms out in front of you.

Por favor, mantenga los brazos a los lados.
Please hold your arms out your sides.

Por favor, haga círculos con los brazos.
Please make circles with you arms.

Por favor, gire la mano hacia el suelo.
Please turn your hand down toward the floor.

Por favor, gire la mano hacia el cielo raso.
Please turn your hand up toward the ceiling.

HANDS/WRISTS

. . . .

Voy a tocarle las manos. Esto puede ser un poco incómodo.
I am going to touch your hands. This may be slightly uncomfortable.

. . . .

EVALUATION

138

Por favor, separe los dedos.
Please spread your fingers out.

Por favor, junte los dedos.
Please bring your fingers together.

Por favor, empuñe.
Please make a fist.

Por favor, mueva los dedos.
Please wiggle your fingers.

Por favor, apriéteme los dedos tan duro como le sea posible.
Please grip my fingers as hard as possible.

Por favor, relaje los dedos.
Please relax your fingers.

Por favor, mueva la muñeca hacia arriba.
Please move your wrist up.

Por favor, mueva la muñeca hacia abajo.
Please move your wrist down.

Por favor, gire la muñeca de un lado para otro.
Please twist your wrist over and back.

Por favor, mueva la muñeca de izquierda a derecha.
Please move your wrist left and right.

STANDING

- -

Por favor, póngase de pie para examinar su postura.

Please stand, so I may examine your posture.

Por favor, aléjese de mí y regrese para poder evaluar su patrón de marcha.

Please walk away from me and then return so I may assess your gait pattern.

Por favor, muéstreme cómo sube y baja gradas.

Please show me how you go up and down stairs.

Por favor, acuclíllese.

Please squat down.

Por favor, inclínese hacia adelante.

Please bend over forward.

Por favor, desplace el peso de su cuerpo hacia la izquierda.

Please shift left.

Por favor, desplace el peso de su cuerpo hacia la derecha.

Please shift right.

Por favor, inclínese hacia atrás.

Please bend backwards.

- -

COORDINATED MOVEMENTS

Por favor, párese en un solo pie.
Please stand on one foot.

Por favor, párese en la punta de los pies.
Please stand up on your toes.

Por favor, acuéstese boca arriba en la estera.
Please lie down on the mat, on your back.

Por favor, acuéstese de lado en la estera.
Please lie down on the mat, on your side.

Por favor, acuéstese boca abajo en la estera.
Please lie down on the mat, on your stomach.

Por favor, dése la vuelta.
Please turn over.

BEDSIDE

Aquí está el botón luminoso para llamar.
Oprima este botón si necesita mi ayuda.
Here is your call light/button. Press this button if you need my help.

Aquí está su orinal o pato (cuña).
Here is your urinal or bed pan.

DIAGNOSTICS

Le voy a tomar la temperatura por vía oral. Por favor, abra la boca
y levante la lengua. Este procedimiento no es doloroso.
I am going to take your oral temperature. Please open your mouth
and lift up your tongue. This procedure will not hurt.

Le voy a tomar la temperatura timpánica. Voy a pegarle un
pequeño dispositivo en el oído. Este procedimiento no es doloroso.
I am going to take your tympanic temperature. I will stick a small device
in your ear. This procedure will not hurt.

Voy a usar un doppler. Por favor, quédese quieto durante
el procedimiento. Este procedimiento no es doloroso.
I am going to use a doppler. Please stay still during the procedure.
This procedure will not hurt.

Un intérprete estará aquí pronto.
An interpreter will be here shortly.

Sé que muchas cosas están pasando alrededor de usted.
No tenga miedo. Todos estamos aquí para ayudarlo.
I know that a lot of things may be happening around you.
Do not be afraid. We are all here to help you.

Tengo que ponerle un collarín cervical alrededor del cuello
para proteger la columna vertebral de una lesión mayor.
Esto puede ser incómodo.
I need to put a cervical collar around your neck to protect your spine
from further injury. This may be uncomfortable.

Tengo que inmovilizarlo sobre este respaldo para proteger la
columna de una lesión. Esto puede ser incómodo.
I need to immobilize your body on a backboard to protect your spine
from injury. This may be uncomfortable.

Le voy a enyesar la extremidad lesionada. Esto puede ser doloroso.
I am going to put a cast on your injured limb. This may be painful.

Lo siento pero no puedo darle líquidos.
I am sorry but I cannot give you liquids.

Lo siento pero no puedo darle comida.
I am sorry but I cannot give you food.

Regresaré en unos momentos para ver cómo se siente.
I will return shortly to check up on you.

Sígame por favor.
Please follow me.

Quédese quieto por favor.
Please be still.

Por favor, relájese.
Please relax.

Estoy aquí para ayudarle.
I am here to help.

Voy a llevarlo a su habitación.
I am going to take you to your room.

Por favor, sígame.
Please follow me.

Por favor, siéntese.
Please sit down.

Por favor, acuéstese.
Please lie down.

Por favor, póngase de pie.
Please stand up.

Por favor, camine hacia mi.
Please walk toward me.

Por favor, métase a la cama.
Please get in bed.

Por favor, siéntese en la silla de ruedas.
Please sit in the wheelchair.

Le voy a administrar oxígeno por la nariz. Esto puede ser un poco incómodo.
I am going to give you oxygen through your nose.
This may be mildly uncomfortable.

Le voy a dar oxígeno a través de esta máscara que se coloca sobre la boca y la nariz. Esto puede ser un poco incómodo.
I am going to give you oxygen through this mask that will will go over your mouth and nose. This may be mildly uncomfortable.

Le voy a colocar un ventilador de presión positiva en modo CPAP o uno de ventilación no invasiva en modo BiPAP. Se siente como si usted hubiera sacado la cabeza por la ventana de un carro en movimiento y será brevemente incómodo.
I am going to put you on a CPAP or BiPAP. It will feel like your head is outside the window of a moving car and will be uncomfortable for a little bit.

Le voy a administrar medicamento mediante un inhalador que calibra la dosis. Este procedimiento no es doloroso.
I am going to give you medication through metered dose inhaler. This will not hurt.

Por favor, exhale totalmente.
Please exhale completely.

Por favor, inhale profundamente.
Please inhale deeply.

Le voy a administrar medicamento mediante un nebulizador. Esto no le va a doler. Por favor, inhale lenta y profundamente.
I am going to give you medication through a nebulizer. This will not hurt. Please inhale slowly and deeply.

Voy a colocarle suero. Sentirá dolor brevemente pero esto es importante hacerlo para poder administrarle medicamentos.

I am going to start an IV. This will hurt briefly but is important so we can give you medication.

Le voy a administrar medicamento en el suero. Tal vez le incomode brevemente.

I am going to give you some medication through your IV. You may feel uncomfortable for a little bit.

Le voy a administrar medicamento con esta jeringa. Tal vez le arda o se sienta incomodo brevemente pero la sensación pasa rápido.

I am going to give you some medication with this needle. This may sting or feel uncomfortable for a little bit but the feeling will pass quickly.

Le voy a sacar una muestra de sangre. Tal vez le incomode brevemente.

I am going to draw a blood sample. It may feel a little uncomfortable.

Voy a colocarle un catéter central. Va a sentir dolor.

I am going to start a central line. This will hurt.

Voy a ganar acceso al catéter central. No va a sentir dolor.

I am going to access your central line. This will not hurt.

Voy a colocarle un catéter central de inserción periférica. Va a sentir dolor.

I am going to start a PICC line. This will hurt.

Voy a colocarle un portacath. Va a sentir dolor.

I am going to start a portacath. This will hurt.

Voy a ganar acceso al portacath. No va a sentir dolor.

I am going to access your portacath. This will not hurt.

Voy a llevarlo a que le realicen una tomografía computarizada.
I am going to take you to get a CT scan.

Por favor, quédese quieto durante el procedimiento.
Este procedimiento no es doloroso.
Please stay still during the procedure. This procedure will not hurt.

Voy a llevarlo a que le tomen una imagen de resonancia magnética.
I am going to take you to get an MRI.

Por favor, quédese quieto durante el procedimiento.
Este procedimiento no es doloroso.
Please stay still during the procedure. This procedure will not hurt.

Voy a llevarlo a que le tomen una radiografía.
I am going to take you to get an X-ray.

Por favor, quédese quieto durante el procedimiento.
Este procedimiento no es doloroso.
Please stay still during the procedure. This procedure will not hurt.

Voy a llevarlo a la Unidad de Cuidados Intensivos (UCI).
I am going to take you to the Intensive Care Unit (ICU).

Voy a llevarlo a otra habitación.
I am going to take you to another room.

Voy a llevarlo de regreso a su habitación.
I am going to take you back to your room.

Muchas gracias por haber venido hoy.
Thank you for seeing us today.

Por favor, llame al (_____) _____ – _____ **el día** _____ / _____
Please call   *on*   **DÍA**   **MES**

para programar una cita de monitoreo para el día _____ / _____ / _____
to schedule a follow up appointment by   **DÍA**   **MES**   **AÑO**

Puede obtener los medicamentos que le recetaron en:
You may fill your prescriptions at:

_____

El número de teléfono de ellos es:
Their phone number is: (_____) _____ – _____

La dirección de ellos es:
Their address is:

_____

Calle (Street)   Apartamento (Apt. #)

_____

Ciudad (City)   Estado (State)   Código Postal (ZIP)

Si tiene preguntas sobre el seguro médico, por favor llame a:
If you have questions regarding medical insurance please call:

(_____) _____ – _____

COMMON NECESSITIES

Use the following images to help determine if the patients are in need of these common necessities.

CAMA
Bed

ALMOHADA
Pillow

COBIJA
Blanket

CONTROL REMOTO
TV Remote

COMPUTADORA
Computer

TELÉFONO
Phone

AGUA
WATER

COMIDA
FOOD

CAFÉ
COFFEE

SERVILLETAS
NAPKINS

CUBIERTOS
SILVERWARE

COMMON NECESSITIES

SILLA DE RUEDAS
Wheelchair

ANDADOR
Walker

BASTON
Cane

SILLA
Chair

INODORO
Toilet

PILA
Sink

LLAVES
Keys

TAXI
Taxi

BASURERO
Trash Can

MONEDERO
Wallet

BOLSA
Purse

GAFAS
Glasses

ABOUT THE AUTHORS

Neil Bobenhouse, MHA, EMT-P

Neil Bobenhouse is a paramedic, entrepreneur, and language enthusiast formerly of the St. Louis City Fire Department. He holds a bachelor's degree in psychology and a master's degree in health administration, both from Saint Louis University. Neil founded Bobenhouse Industries with the vision to create real-world solutions for the healthcare industry.

PHRASEBOOK CONTRIBUTORS

James A. Bobenhouse, MD
Board Certified Neurology and Vascular Neurology
Bryan Medical Center and St. Elizabeth Regional Medical Center
Stroke Center Medical Director

Mark Levine, MD, FACEP
Assistant Professor, Emergency Medicine
Washington University School of Medicine
Barnes-Jewish Hospital

Dean C. Meenach, RN, BSN, CEN, CCRN, CPEN, EMT-P
Director of EMS Education, Mineral Area College

Casey Regen, RN, TNCC

Morgan Grubbe, PT, DPT

All translations by International Institute of Saint Louis Language Services
Graphic Design & Illustrations by Andrea Molina
Previous Graphic Design & Illustrations by Ben Gathard

ACKNOWLEDGMENTS

The St. Louis City Fire Department
Washington University
Barnes-Jewish Hospital
Andrea Alameda, Shawn Bittle, Guy Jennings, Bhavin Mehta, Doug Randell, Matt Sleet, and Galen Taylor. Mike Barnes, Mike Beckenholdt, Jheree Coleman, Jack Douglas, Jeff Glorioso, Pam Miller, Ed Monser, Steve Ponzar, Dr. David Tan, Michelle Vaught, and Chris Yacula. Sarah Barekzai, Byron Beiermann, Stav Dor, Jake Flemming, Dr. Sai Iyer, Will Massanet, Laura Walsh, and Grace Pryor.

CPSIA information can be obtained
at www.ICGtesting.com
Printed in the USA
FSOW04n1824230317
32198FS